eKNOW 2025

The Seventeenth International Conference on Information, Process, and Knowledge Management

May 18 - 22, 2025

Nice, France

eKNOW 2025 Editors

Susan Gauch, University of Arkansas, USA

Samia Aitouche, University Batna 2, Algeria

Printed from e-media with permission by:

Curran Associates, Inc.
57 Morehouse Lane
Red Hook, NY 12571

Some format issues inherent in the e-media version may also appear in this print version.

Printed with permission by Curran Associates, Inc. (2025)

International Academy, Research, and Industry Association (IARIA)
412 Derby Way
Wilmington, DE 19810

Phone: (408) 893-6407
Fax: (408) 527-6351

petre@iaria.org

Additional copies of this publication are available from:

Curran Associates, Inc.
57 Morehouse Lane
Red Hook, NY 12571 USA
Phone: 845-758-0400
Fax: 845-758-2633
Email: curran@proceedings.com
Web: www.proceedings.com

Table of Contents

Heuristic Search Using Language Models and Reinforcement Learning 1
Carolina Carvalho and Paulo Quaresma

Optimizing Resource Management in Algerian Traditional Brick Manufacturing (SNG) Using Blockchain-Based Smart Contracts with Solidity 13
Aimene Boughrira, Samia Aitouche, El Hocine Grabsi, Hichem Aouag, Kamel Taouririt, and Khireddine Bourmel

VAULT: Verified Access Control for LLM-Based Knowledge Graph Querying 21
Maximilian Stabler, Tobias Muller, Frank Koster, and Chris Langdon

Stance-Conditioned Modeling for Rumor Verification 30
Gibson Nkhata and Susan Gauch

Defect Prevention Review by Process Relationship Matrix 37
Shuichiro Yamamoto

Measuring Tacit Knowledge Hiding in IT Consulting Firms 41
Jason Triche

Fair Learning for Bias Mitigation and Quality Optimization in Paper Recommendation 43
Uttamasha Anjally Oyshi and Susan Gauch

ColBERT-Based User Profiles for Personalized Information Retrieval 51
Aleena Ahmad, Gibson Nkhata, Abdul Rafay Bajwa, Hannah Marsico, Bryan Le, and Susan Gauch

Identification and Characterization of Content Traps in YouTube Recommendation Network 59
Monoarul Bhuiyan and Nitin Agarwal

eKNOW 2025

Forward

The Seventeenth International Conference on Information, Process, and Knowledge Management (eKNOW 2025), held between May 18th, 2025, and May 22nd, 2025, in Nice, France, continued a series of events covering the complexity of the current systems, the diversity of the data, and the challenges for mental representation and understanding of environmental structure and behavior.

Capturing, representing, and manipulating knowledge was and still is a fascinating and extremely useful challenge from both a theoretical and practical perspective. Using validated knowledge for information and process management and for decision support mechanisms raised a series of questions the eKNOW 2025 conference was aimed at.

The event provided a forum where researchers were able to present recent research results and new research problems and directions related to them. The topics covered aspects from knowledge fundamentals to more specialized topics such as process analysis and modeling, management systems, semantics processing and ontology.

We take here the opportunity to warmly thank all the members of the eKNOW 2025 technical program committee, as well as all the reviewers. The creation of such a high-quality conference program would not have been possible without their involvement. We also kindly thank all the authors who dedicated much of their time and effort to contribute to eKNOW 2025. We truly believe that, thanks to all these efforts, the final conference program consisted of top-quality contributions. We also thank the members of the eKNOW 2025 organizing committee for their help in handling the logistics of this event.

We hope that eKNOW 2025 was a successful international forum for the exchange of ideas and results between academia and industry for the promotion of progress in the field of information, process, and knowledge management.

eKNOW 2025 Chairs

eKNOW 2025 Steering Committee
Susan Gauch, University of Arkansas, USA
Samia Aitouche, Laboratory of Automation and Manufacturing (LAP), University Batna 2, Algeria
Roy Oberhauser, Aalen University, Germany

eKNOW 2025 Publicity Chairs
José Miguel Jiménez, Universitat Politècnica de València, Spain
Francisco Javier Díaz Blasco, Universitat Politècnica de València, Spain
Ali Ahmad, Universitat Politècnica de València, Spain
Sandra Viciano Tudela, Universitat Politècnica de València, Spain
Laura Garcia, Universidad Politécnica de Cartagena, Spain

eKNOW 2025
Committee

eKNOW 2025 Steering Committee

Susan Gauch, University of Arkansas, USA
Samia Aitouche, Laboratory of Automation and Manufacturing (LAP), University Batna 2, Algeria
Roy Oberhauser, Aalen University, Germany

eKNOW 2025 Publicity Chairs

José Miguel Jiménez, Universitat Politècnica de València, Spain
Francisco Javier Díaz Blasco, Universitat Politècnica de València, Spain
Ali Ahmad, Universitat Politècnica de València, Spain
Sandra Viciano Tudela, Universitat Politècnica de València, Spain
Laura Garcia, Universidad Politécnica de Cartagena, Spain

eKNOW 2025 Technical Program Committee

Rocío Abascal Mena, Universidad Autónoma Metropolitana - Cuajimalpa, Mexico City, Mexico
Malak A. Abdullah, Jordan University of Science and Technology, Jordan
Marie-Hélène Abel, Sorbonne universités - Université de technologie de Compiègne, France
Awais Adnan, Institute of Management Sciences Peshawar, Pakistan
Nitin Agarwal, University of Arkansas at Little Rock, USA
Abdullah Fathi Ahmed, University Paderborn, Germany
Samia Aitouche, University Batna 2, Algeria
Arnulfo Alanis, Instituto Tecnológico de Tijuana | Tecnológico Nacional de México, Mexico
Mohammad T. Alshammari, University of Hail, Saudi Arabia
Bráulio Alturas, Instituto Universitário de Lisboa (ISCTE-IUL) | ISTAR-Iscte (University Institute of Lisbon), Portugal
Gil Ad Ariely, Lauder School of Government, Diplomacy and Strategy - Interdisciplinary Center Herzliya (IDC), Israel
Mohamed Anis Bach Tobji, ESEN – University of Manouba | LARODEC Laboratory – ISG of Tunis, Tunisia
Mário Antunes, Polytechnic of Leiria, Portugal
Jorge Manuel Azevedo Santos, Universidade de Évora, Portugal
Michal Baczynski, University of Silesia in Katowice, Poland
Zbigniew Banaszak, Koszalin University of Technology, Poland
Basel Bani-Ismail, Oman College of Management and Technology, Oman
Dusan Barac, University of Belgrade, Serbia
Peter Bellström, Karlstad University, Sweden
Hajer Ben Othman, National school of computer science - University of Manouba, Tunisia
Asmaa Benghabrit, Moulay Ismaïl University, Meknès, Morocco
José Alberto Benítez Andrades, University of León, Spain
Julita Bermejo-Alonso, Universidad Isabel I, Spain
Shankar Biradar, Indian Institute of Information Technology Dharwad, India
Karsten Boehm, University of Applied Sciences, Kufstein, Austria

Zorica Bogdanovic, University of Belgrade, Serbia
Amel Borgi, LIPAH, Université de Tunis El Manar, Tunisia
Gregory Bourguin, LISIC | Université Littoral Côte d'Opale(ULCO), France
Loris Bozzato, FBK-Irst | Fondazione Bruno Kessler, Trento, Italy
Bénédicte Bucher, University Gustave Eiffel | ENS | IGN | LaSTIG, France
Ozgu Can, Ege University, Turkey
Lorenzo Capra, State University of Milano, Italy
Massimiliano Caramia, University of Rome "Tor Vergata", Italy
Vítor Carvalho, 2Ai-EST-IPCA / Algoritmi Research Center - Minho University, Portugal
Dickson K.W. Chiu, The University of Hong Kong, Hong Kong
Ritesh Chugh, Central Queensland University, Australia
Anacleto Correia, Naval Academy, Portugal
Miguel Couceiro, University of Lorraine | CNRS | Inria Nancy G.E. | Loria, France
Juan Pablo D'Amato, Universidad Nacional del Centro de la PRov (UNCPBA) / CONICET, Argentina
Anca Daniela Ionita, National University of Science and Technology POLITEHNICA Bucharest, Romania
Gustavo de Assis Costa, Federal Institute of Education, Science and Technology of Goiás, Brazil / LIAAD - INESC TEC, Portugal
Joaquim De Moura, University of A Coruña, Spain
Cláudio de Souza Baptista, University of Campina Grande, Brazil
Sylvie Despres, Université Sorbonne Paris Nord, France
Giuseppe A. Di Lucca, University of Sannio | RCOST (Research Center on Software Technology), Italy
Vasiliki Diamantopoulou, University of the Aegean, Greece
Mihaela Dinsoreanu, Technical University of Cluj-Napoca, Romania
Gokila Dorai, Augusta University, USA
Tomasz Dudek, Maritime University of Szczecin, Poland
Sourav Dutta, Ramapo College of New Jersey, USA
Tygran Dzhuguryan, Maritime University of Szczecin, Poland
Tome Eftimov, Jožef Stefan Institute, Ljubljana, Slovenia / Stanford University, Palo Alto, USA
Kemele M. Endris, L3S Research Center, Hannover, Germany
Fairouz Fakhfakh, Universiy of Sfax, Tunisia
Lamine Faty, Université Assane Seck de Ziguinchor, Senegal
Amélia Ferreira da Silva, Centre for Organizational and Social Studies of Porto Polytechnic, Portugal
Joan Francesc Fondevila, Universitat de Girona / Universitat Pompeu Fabra, Spain
Igor Garcia Ballhausen Sampaio, Instituto de Computação (UFF), Brazil
Susan Gauch, University of Arkansas, USA
Dipesh Gautam, Institute for Intelligent Systems (IIS) | The University of Memphis, USA
Markus Grube, VOQUZ IT Solutions GmbH, Germany
Teresa Guarda, Universidad Estatal Peninsula Santa Elena - UPSE, Ecuador
Michael Guckert, Technische Hochschule Mittelhessen, Germany
Carolina Guerini, Cattaneo University Castellanza (Varese) / Sda Bocconi, Milan, Italy
Gunadi Gunadi, Gajayana University, Malang, Indonesia
Juncal Gutiérrez-Artacho, Universidad de Granada, Spain
Mounira Harzallah, LS2N | University of Nantes, France
Hussein Y. Hazimeh, Al Maaref University & Lebanese University, Lebanon
Manuel Herranz, Pangeanic, Spain
Stijn Hoppenbrouwers, HAN University of Applied Sciences, Arnhem / Radboud University, Nijmegen, Netherlands
Syeda Sumbul Hossain, Daffodil International University, Bangladesh

Daniel O'Leary, University of Southern California, USA
Eva Oliveira, 2Ai Polytechnic Institute of Cávado and Ave, Barcelos, Portugal
Wiesław Paja, University of Rzeszów, Poland
João Paulo Costa, University of Coimbra, Portugal
Jean-Éric Pelet, EMLV and SKEMA Business Schools, France
Rúben Pereira, ISCTE, Portugal
António Miguel Pesqueira, Bavarian Nordic, Denmark
Sylvain Piechowiak, Université Polytechnique Hauts-de-France, France
Salviano Pinto Soares, University of Trás-os-Montes and Alto Douro (UTAD), Portugal
Rodica Potolea, Technical University of Cluj-Napoca, Romania
Adam Przybylek, Gdansk University of Technology, Poland
Paulo Quaresma, University of Évora, Portugal
Lukasz Radlinski, West Pomeranian University of Technology in Szczecin, Poland
Enayat Rajabi, Cape Breton University, Canada
Arsénio Reis, Universidade de Trás-os-Montes e Alto Douro, Portugal
Simona Riurean, University of Petrosani, Romania
Irene Rivera-Trigueros, University of Granada, Spain
Mário Rodrigues, University of Aveiro, Portugal
Polina Rozenshtein, Aalto University, Helsinki, Finland
Inès Saad, Amiens Business School & University Picardie Jules Verne, France
Tanik Saikh, Kalinga Institute of Industrial Technology, India
Virginie Sans, INRISA/IRISA Université of Rennes 1, France
Lalia Saoudi, Msila University, Algeria
Antonio Sarasa Cabezuelo, Universidad Complutense de Madrid, Spain
Hartmut Schweizer, Institute for Applied Computer Science - TU Dresden, Germany
Filippo Sciarrone, ROMA TRE University, Italy
Marcelo Seido Nagano, University of São Paulo, Brazil
Houcine Senoussi, Quartz laboratory - EISTI, Cergy, France
Luciano Serafini, FBK - Fondazione Bruno Kessler, Italy
Nuno Silva, ISEP - IPP (School of Engineering - Polytechnic of Porto), Portugal
Thoudam Doren Singh, National Institute of Technology Silchar, India
Andrzej M.J. Skulimowski, AGH University of Science and Technology, Krakow, Poland
Koen Smit, Hogeschool Utrecht -Institute for ICT, Netherlands
Christophe Soares, Universidade Fernando Pessoa, Portugal
Darielson Souza, Federal University of Ceará (UFC), Brazil
Gautam Srivastava, Brandon University, Canada
Deborah Stacey, University of Guelph, Canada
Efstathios Stamatatos, University of the Aegean, Greece
Abel Suing, Universidad Técnica Particular de Loja, Ecuador
Marta Silvia Tabares, Universidad EAFIT, Medellín, Colombia
Nelson Tenório, UniCesumar, Brazil
Takao Terano, Chiba University of Commerce / Tokyo Institute of Technology / University of Tsukuba, Japan
Giorgio Terracina, University of Calabria, Italy
Michele Tomaiuolo, Università di Parma, Italy
George Tambouratzis, ILSP/Athena Research Centre, Greece
Christos Troussas, Department of Informatics - University of Piraeus, Greece
Esteban Vázquez Cano, Universidad Nacional de Educación a Distancia (UNED), Spain

Marco Viviani, University of Milano-Bicocca, Italy
Ruixiao Wang, Yale University, USA
Yingxu Wang, University of Calgary, Canada
Hans Weigand, Tilburg University, Netherlands
Rihito Yaegashi, Kagawa University, Japan
Shuichiro Yamamoto, International Professional University in Nagoya, Japan
Brahmi Zaki, Taibah University, KSA
Cecilia Zanni-Merk, INSA Rouen Normandie, France
Elmoukhtar Zemmouri, Moulay Ismail University, Meknes, Morocco
Qiang Zhu, University of Michigan - Dearborn, USA
Beata Zielosko, University of Silesia in Katowice, Poland
Magdalena Zioło, University of Szczecin, Poland
Mounir Zrigui, Faculté des Sciences de Monastir, Tunisia

Copyright Information

For your reference, this is the text governing the copyright release for material published by IARIA.

The copyright release is a transfer of publication rights, which allows IARIA and its partners to drive the dissemination of the published material. This allows IARIA to give articles increased visibility via distribution, inclusion in libraries, and arrangements for submission to indexes.

I, the undersigned, declare that the article is original, and that I represent the authors of this article in the copyright release matters. If this work has been done as work-for-hire, I have obtained all necessary clearances to execute a copyright release. I hereby irrevocably transfer exclusive copyright for this material to IARIA. I give IARIA permission or reproduce the work in any media format such as, but not limited to, print, digital, or electronic. I give IARIA permission to distribute the materials without restriction to any institutions or individuals. I give IARIA permission to submit the work for inclusion in article repositories as IARIA sees fit.

I, the undersigned, declare that to the best of my knowledge, the article is does not contain libelous or otherwise unlawful contents or invading the right of privacy or infringing on a proprietary right.

Following the copyright release, any circulated version of the article must bear the copyright notice and any header and footer information that IARIA applies to the published article.

IARIA grants royalty-free permission to the authors to disseminate the work, under the above provisions, for any academic, commercial, or industrial use. IARIA grants royalty-free permission to any individuals or institutions to make the article available electronically, online, or in print.

IARIA acknowledges that rights to any algorithm, process, procedure, apparatus, or articles of manufacture remain with the authors and their employers.

I, the undersigned, understand that IARIA will not be liable, in contract, tort (including, without limitation, negligence), pre-contract or other representations (other than fraudulent misrepresentations) or otherwise in connection with the publication of my work.

Exception to the above is made for work-for-hire performed while employed by the government. In that case, copyright to the material remains with the said government. The rightful owners (authors and government entity) grant unlimited and unrestricted permission to IARIA, IARIA's contractors, and IARIA's partners to further distribute the work.

Heuristic Search Using Language Models and Reinforcement Learning

Carolina Carvalho, and Paulo Quaresma
Department of Computer Science
University of Évora Évora, Portugal
e-mail: carolina.rcxc@gmail.com | pq@uevora.pt

***Abstract*—This article extends the applicability domain of language models to problems where candidate solutions can be expressed as an encoded integer sequence. Considering this sequence, language models can operate in the neural machine translation setting and leverage their optimization power for heuristic search techniques. Reinforcement Learning (RL) is applied to Language Models (LM), regardless of whether character-level or word-level models are used as a basis. To stabilize the learning, several approaches are explored, including functional and architectural decoupling. The framework is then applied to two combinatorial problems, namely the Traveling Salesman Problem benchmark and Neural Architecture Search, which is used to generate a hierarchical (tree-based) text classifier where the blocks are inspired by the InceptionV1 architecture. The decoupling results are the main contribution of this paper, easing the RL and LM stabilization requirements while expanding the resolution domain beyond Markov Decision Processes to non-causal normative heuristic problems, such as Neural Architecture Search (NAS).**

Keywords-Heuristic Optimization; Reinforcement Leaning; Language Model; Task Semantic Segmentation; Artificial Neural Network.

I. INTRODUCTION

Regarding the Natural Language Processing domain, the auto-encoder Language Models are typically trained on a large corpus. To evaluate the language model, the pretrained encoder, along with a custom decoder tailored to the downstream task, is then fine-tuned to address the specific task. The encoder part of the language model retains knowledge and maps semantics to a reduced latent dimension. This learned mapping keeps, in the encoder's weights, general type features, such as how to speak a language. This work explores the language model's encoder capability to retain the semantics of other problems beyond merely speaking a language. Additionally, the generative capability of language models is examined.

There are instances where the intention is to model the dataset's probability density function rather than the data itself; for example, in generative models, the goal is to generate data similar to the dataset. To achieve this objective, variational models come into play, specifically Variational Auto-Encoders (VAE) [1]–[11] and Generative Adversarial Network (GAN) architectures [12]–[18]. The GAN architectures use a Generator and a Discriminator network and employ min-max training. During training, the generator network produces data samples of better quality at each time step to trick the discriminator, which learns to distinguish real data from fake data generated by the Generator network. In this manner, both networks engaged in min-max training learn to perform their respective tasks. The Generator produces more realistic data samples as the Discriminator becomes increasingly difficult to deceive. In terms of VAEs, these models approximate the dataset's probability density function by modeling its parameters [19] or by assigning an odds to each output [20], generating data from the random variable where each output holds the model's estimated odds. The resulting binary text classifier positioning of a dataset, this work posits that any problem for which the solutions can be encoded in an integer sequence can also be addressed in a generative manner. It is essential to assert that the optimization goal is expressible through a heuristic function, akin to the fitness function in the context of Genetic Algorithms (GAs) [21]–[30]. Heuristic search using Language Models suffers from a lack of exploration due to the well-known difficulty of stabilizing complex neural models when trained using Reinforcement Learning. Traditional issues include training convergence and subsequent hyperparameter tuning. Furthermore, RL is usually applied sequentially to causal problems. This paper proposes decoupling-based RL training techniques and network architecture design principles that enable the application of RL to new problem types, as well as the incorporation of Language Models' feature capture capabilities to address problems beyond linguistic ones. Considering the sequence encoding of the candidate solutions generated by the language model, an ontology must be defined to encode and serialize the candidates, allowing the architectures to generate data structures and refine them during training, similar to a GAN training setting. In contrast to traditional Heuristic Search methods, where the candidate solution can be an array of various degrees of freedom in the problem (e.g., variables in a multivariate optimization problem), language models can capture the data structure or ontology with the help of special characters. These characters are used in the sequence encoding, signaling the evaluation methodology to build and assess a diversity of data structures. This capability is referred to in this paper as Semantic Encoding. It is applied to the Neural Architecture Search downstream problem. The rest of this paper is organized as follows: II. Related Work, III. Semantic Encoding, IV. Proposed Architectures, V. Reinforcement Learning as a Search Methodology, VI. Decoupled Asynchronous Advantage Actor-Critic, VII. Decoupled Soft Q-Learning, VIII. Decoupling's Mathematical Formalization, IX. Proposed Training Formulation, X. Accessed Problems, XI. Results, XII. Error Analysis. Finally, the paper concludes with XIII. Conclusions and Future Work.

II. Related Work

The proposed heuristic search relates mainly to evolutionary algorithms, such as Genetic Algorithms. The adopted models are neural Language Models, and the training is based on Reinforcement Learning. In this section, all the aforementioned methods are detailed. Evolutionary algorithms can be seen as heuristic search engines in the sense that they generate candidate solutions, which are evaluated on the fly using a heuristic function, such as the fitness function in the case of Genetic Algorithms. Neural Language Models (LMs) are used for language modeling [31]–[38]. They learn meaningful features from text data through embedding generation techniques. When an LM is used in the context of Neural Machine Translation [36], [39]–[44], LMs can be viewed as generative models because they generate tokens that, when decoded, are words in the target language domain. This problem can be generalized into a Sequence2Sequence problem when considering the same language model architecture generating a sequence with a different semantic encoding than target language tokens, always restricted to a differentiable loss function. Neural Machine Translation (NMT) architectures are generative by nature because they produce tokens in the model's target language, although their training typically requires a differentiable loss function that might not accurately express the training goals. The same occurs in NAS tasks, where the primary objective is to increasingly enhance the candidate network's performance metric. In [45], a Recurrent Neural Network (RNN) is trained using Reinforcement Learning (RL) with the candidate network's performance almost directly serving as the reward function, employing various techniques to reduce the training's variance and facilitate learning through the described method. To relax the differentiable metric constraint, a new type of training is necessary; this is where Reinforcement Learning (RL) becomes relevant. RL techniques are primarily based on Markov Decision Processes (MDPs). Several training approaches attempt to optimize non-differentiable metrics in a deep model, such as surrogate losses [46], minimum risk training [47], and reinforcement learning [45]. All these training methodologies have their limitations: surrogate losses and reinforcement learning are difficult to stabilize, and minimum risk training is too computationally expensive when applied to a language model like an NMT architecture. Focusing on RL training, this article explores methods to stabilize the training and establish a robust optimization framework.

III. Semantic Encoding

Sequence semantic encoding is one of the core subjects in this proposal. When applied to the sequence generated by a Neural Machine Translation model, the problem can be transposed into an optimization problem where the candidates can be encoded as a sequence of integers [45]. The candidate solutions' meta-format can be a single value or a sequence of values, depending on the downstream problem. Special characters such as separators or sequence terminators can also be used to help specify the solution's evaluator behavior. The optimization problem structure that this kind of semantic encoding enables is a heuristic search, since the candidate solution's quality is evaluated by a reward function that can be non-differentiable, and its value can be generated during the search execution.

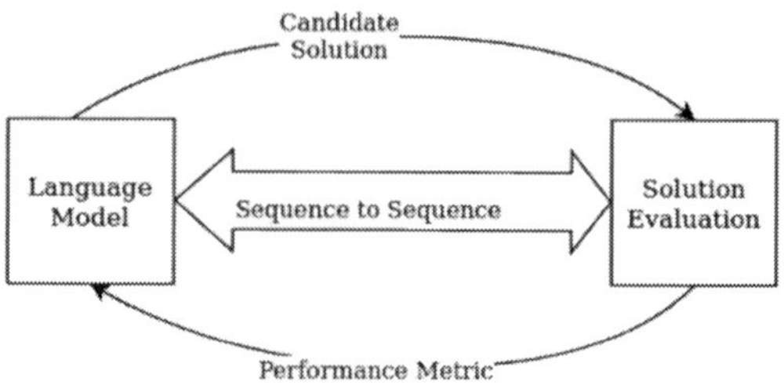

Figure 1. Heuristic search architecture.

For example, in order to access the Neural Architecture Search (NAS) problem using the proposed technique, the sequence can be the Network Structure Code (NSC), which encodes the candidate neural network hyperparameters. The network is then built and trained so that the performance metric can be extracted and the candidate sequence evaluated. Figure 1 highlights the proposed heuristic search architecture.

IV. Proposed Architectures

Depending on the nature of the problem, it can be beneficial to generate the sequence iteratively or through composition. As this article's subject is the usage of language models in optimization problems, and language models can encode semantics based on characters or words, both approaches will be explored further.

With the RL training enabled by the decoupling, based on unitary and semantically segmented tasks assigned to unitary model parts, the proposed architectures consist of two models inspired by character-level and word-level language models, respectively. With this training possibility, these models' generalization capability, as well as the proposed modeling principle, will be assessed.

A. *Char-Conv with DeepQNet-Policy Learning*

Starting from the model proposed in [48], two output kernels were used to decouple the tasks into position and value generation. In this way, one model pair, Q-Network and Policy-Net, is used to compose the candidate sequence. Regarding the Traveling Salesman Problem, a benchmark problem, the proposed training setting works without issues. When considering the Neural Architecture Search problem, the reward signal presents high variance and the training did not converge to zero. In addressing this problem, two changes were made: entropy regularization was added, and the output activation function was changed to linear so that the model output is interpreted as log probabilities for each output position.

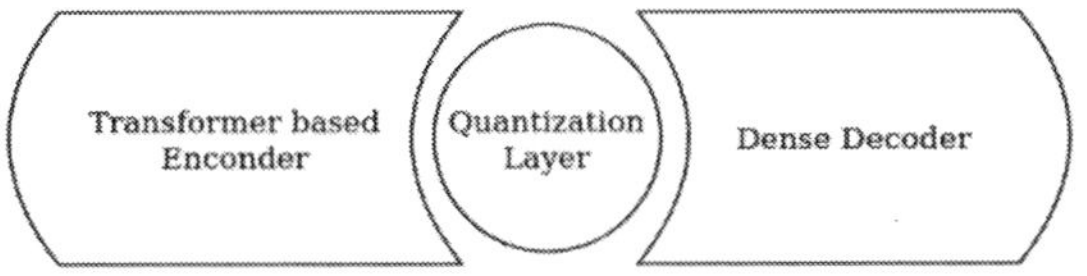

Figure 2. Vector Quantized Variational Auto-Encoder proposed architecture. The encoder comes from the Transformer architecture, the quantization layer from [20], and the decoder is made of stacked dense layers.

B. Transformer-based Vector Quantized Variational Auto-Encoder with Asynchronous Advantage Actor Critic

The word-level model is based on the Transformer architecture proposed in [49], which includes both the Transformer encoder and decoder architectures, along with the vector quantization layer proposed in [20]. This Vector Quantized Variational Autoencoder (VQ-VAE) architecture was decoupled as well; however, in this case, its outputs correspond to the actor and the critic. The actor outputs log probabilities for the possible actions of the RL agent, and the critic rates the inputs. Maintaining the sequence composition decoupling strategy, two models are employed to compose the target sequence. Once again, one model specializes in generating the position, while the second model generates the value to be assigned. Figure 2 illustrates the architecture utilized for the VQ-VAE.

V. Reinforcement Learning as a Search Methodology

Since the search for optimal solutions is guided by reinforcement learning, the model generates multiple candidate solutions and iteratively improves them based on feedback. A heuristic evaluation function $g : \mathcal{Y} \to \mathbb{R}$ assigns a quality score to candidate solutions, serving as a reward signal:

$$R(y) = g(y). \tag{1}$$

Given any problem where the solution space $\mathcal{Y}$ is structured as integer sequences, the proposed methodology guarantees:

- **Expressibility**: The model $\hat{f}_\theta$ can learn to generate valid sequences from $\mathcal{X}$ using neural networks that are trained on $\mathcal{D}$.
- **Optimization Capability**: The reinforcement learning-based search ensures that generated solutions are iteratively improved using $g(y)$.
- **Generalization**: The auto-regressive nature of the model allows it to generate variable-length solutions applicable to different instances of the problem since a special character can be used as a sequence terminator.

Thus, for any integer-encoded problem, the formulation is sufficient to obtain high-quality solutions through iterative refinement. The proposed formulation applies to a wide range of problems where solutions are represented as integer sequences, including:

- Combinatorial optimization problems (e.g., the Traveling Salesman Problem, Knapsack Problem).
- Scheduling and planning tasks where actions are encoded as integer sequences.
- Code synthesis and symbolic regression.
- Game strategies with discrete action spaces.
- Non-sequential problems that benefit from value-position decoupling.

For any such problem, the integer-encoded representation ensures that the model can map problem instances to structured sequences and refine them over iterations using reinforcement learning. The search methodology follows a reinforcement learning-based approach such as DQN-PL [50], [51], A3C [52], and SoftQ-Learning [53]. The exploration methodology is epsilon-greedy for all the approaches. The different training methodologies are described in the next subsections.

VI. Decoupled Asynchronous Advantage Actor Critic

The main concept in decoupling is to create a problem feature extraction core and decoupled output decoders to model the output value according to the problem's required output. For example, in the VQ-VAE with the A3C training case, the same model generates the action and its corresponding critic value. To generate a sequence, two models with the specified decoupling are used: one generates the position of the new element, and the second generates its value. The resulting sequence is then updated and iteratively refined. Next, the formal formulation of this kind of decoupling is provided.

A. Policy and Value Functions

Let S be the state space, A be the action space, and $P(s'|s,a)$ be the transition probability. The reward function is defined as $R(s,a,p)$, where p is the selected position.

The policy consists of two independent components:

$$\pi(a|s;\theta_a) \quad \text{and} \quad \pi(p|s;\theta_p) \tag{2}$$

where:

- $\pi(a|s;\theta_a)$ selects an action based on state s.
- $\pi(p|s;\theta_p)$ selects a position based on state s.

The value functions are defined as:

$$V_{\text{act}}(s;\theta_v) = \mathbb{E}\left[R(s,a,p) + \gamma V_{\text{act}}(s')\right] \tag{3}$$

$$V_{\text{pos}}(s;\theta_p) = \mathbb{E}\left[R(s,a,p) + \gamma V_{\text{pos}}(s')\right] \tag{4}$$

B. Exploration-Exploitation Strategy

The exploration rate for both action and position selection follows an epsilon-greedy decay:

$$\epsilon_a(t+1) = \max(\epsilon_a(t)\cdot d, \epsilon_{\min}) \tag{5}$$

$$\epsilon_p(t) = \epsilon_a(t) \tag{6}$$

where d is the decay factor and $\epsilon_{\min}$ is the minimum exploration rate.

C. Advantage Function and Returns

The advantage function for actions is given by:

$$A_{\text{act}}(s,a) = r + \gamma V_{\text{act}}(s') - V_{\text{act}}(s) \tag{7}$$

The advantage function for positions is:

$$A_{\text{pos}}(s,p) = r + \gamma V_{\text{pos}}(s') - V_{\text{pos}}(s) \tag{8}$$

The discounted return at timestep t is:

$$G_t = \sum_{k=0}^{T-t} \gamma^k R(s_{t+k}, a_{t+k}, p_{t+k}) \tag{9}$$

The returns are then normalized:

$$\hat{G}_t = \frac{G_t - \mu(G)}{\sigma(G) + \epsilon} \tag{10}$$

D. Loss Functions

The critic losses for action and position value networks are:

$$L_{\text{critic-act}} = \sum_t \left(A_{\text{act}}(s_t, a_t)\right)^2 \tag{11}$$

$$L_{\text{critic-pos}} = \sum_t \left(A_{\text{pos}}(s_t, p_t)\right)^2 \tag{12}$$

The actor losses are:

$$L_{\text{actor-act}} = -\sum_t \log \pi(a_t|s_t) A_{\text{act}}(s_t, a_t) \tag{13}$$

$$L_{\text{actor-pos}} = -\sum_t \log \pi(p_t|s_t) A_{\text{pos}}(s_t, p_t) \tag{14}$$

The total losses are:

$$L_{\text{total-act}} = L_{\text{actor-act}} + L_{\text{critic-act}} \tag{15}$$

$$L_{\text{total-pos}} = L_{\text{actor-pos}} + L_{\text{critic-pos}} \tag{16}$$

E. Gradient Updates

Gradients for action and position networks are computed separately:

$$\nabla_{\theta_a} L_{\text{total-act}} = \sum_t \nabla_{\theta_a} L_{\text{total-act}} \tag{17}$$

$$\nabla_{\theta_p} L_{\text{total-pos}} = \sum_t \nabla_{\theta_p} L_{\text{total-pos}} \tag{18}$$

These gradients are applied using an optimizer:

$$\theta_a \leftarrow \theta_a - \alpha \nabla_{\theta_a} L_{\text{total-act}} \tag{19}$$

$$\theta_p \leftarrow \theta_p - \alpha \nabla_{\theta_p} L_{\text{total-pos}} \tag{20}$$

where α is the learning rate.

This content was generated with the help of generative artificial intelligence [54].

VII. Decoupled SoftQ-Learning

Regarding the CharConv model in the NAS problem assessment, it was not possible to stabilize the training using the traditional DQN-PL approach. In the NAS setting, it was found beneficial for training stability to use stochastic outputs followed by a random experiment with the model's predicted output odds to generate the predicted action. To help stabilize the training in a stochastic environment, entropy regularization was employed.

Concerning the decoupling technique used in this context, two models were utilized. One model features a CharConv core and two decoupled outputs: one for value and another for the position of the new element in sequence generation. The second model is the target network, which generates the stochastic SoftQ-values for each output.

Additionally, an epsilon-greedy exploration strategy was applied in conjunction with an experience replay buffer. The proposed SoftQ-Learning approach uses a different decoupling when compared to the method presented in the previous section. This is specified in the subsequent subsections.

A. State and Action Representation

Let $s \in \mathcal{S}$ be the state space and $a \in \mathcal{A}$ be the action space. Additionally, let $p \in \mathcal{P}$ denote the position selection space. The agent selects both an action and a position at each time step.

B. Soft Q-Function

Define the Q-function as:

$$Q(s,a,p) = Q_{\text{action}}(s,a) + Q_{\text{position}}(s,p). \tag{21}$$

This decoupling allows independent learning of action and position values.

C. Soft Q-Learning Update Rule

The update rule follows the soft Bellman equation:

$$\begin{aligned} Q_{\text{action}}(s,a) &\leftarrow (1-\alpha) Q_{\text{action}}(s,a) \\ &+ \alpha \left[r + \gamma\tau \log \sum_{a'} \exp\left(\frac{Q_{\text{action}}(s',a')}{\tau} \right) \right], \end{aligned} \tag{22}$$

$$\begin{aligned} Q_{\text{position}}(s,p) &\leftarrow (1-\alpha) Q_{\text{position}}(s,p) \\ &+ \alpha \left[r + \gamma\tau \log \sum_{p'} \exp\left(\frac{Q_{\text{position}}(s',p')}{\tau} \right) \right]. \end{aligned} \tag{23}$$

where:

- α is the learning rate,
- γ is the discount factor,
- τ is the temperature parameter for soft Q-learning,
- r is the received reward,
- s' is the next state.

D. Action and Position Selection

The action and position are selected using the softmax policy:

$$P(a|s) = \frac{\exp(Q_{\text{action}}(s,a)/\tau)}{\sum_{a'} \exp(Q_{\text{action}}(s,a')/\tau)}, \tag{24}$$

$$P(p|s) = \frac{\exp(Q_{\text{position}}(s,p)/\tau)}{\sum_{p'} \exp(Q_{\text{position}}(s,p')/\tau)}. \tag{25}$$

This formulation [55] allows efficient and structured learning by decoupling position and value, improving performance in reinforcement learning tasks that require both action selection and spatial positioning.

In the next section the position-value decoupling for integer-based sequences is formalized.

VIII. Decoupling's Mathematical Formalization

When considering an iteratively generated sequence, in which the elements are generated one after another, the position is fixed and incremental, which implies causality in the sequence generation. By decoupling the functionality into position generation and value generation, thereby composing a single sequence (RL state), it is possible to break the causality implication and still utilize the reinforcement learning capability of optimizing heuristic functions. In this article, the decoupling is achieved at an architectural level; in a multi-branch architecture, each output branch is responsible for one single decoupled task in the non-causal sequence generation. To optimize a single sequence using two models, the state must be shared, and the RL techniques must still be applied to each model, utilizing separate optimizers guided by the same resulting reward.

In incremental sequence generation, this type of sequence generation allows for imposing causality in the RL agent's behavior, leading to a succession of actions generated throughout the training. Regarding compositional sequence generation, where the problem focus is to generate a candidate answer encoded in the sequence rather than a set of actions, decoupling can come into play to divide and conquer the generation problem into two sub-problems, enabling the composition of the sequence without needing to condition on the previous actions.

To extend RL beyond causal MDPs, we decompose the Q-function as follows:

$$Q(s,a) = P(s) + A(s,a), \tag{26}$$

where:

- $P(s) = \mathbb{E}[R|s]$ is the **position value**, which captures the expected reward at state s independent of actions.
- $A(s,a) = Q(s,a) - P(s)$ is the **advantage function**, representing the additional benefit of taking action a beyond merely being in state s.

If actions have no influence (a fully non-causal setting), then $A(s,a) = 0$, reducing RL to pure statistical inference:

$$V(s) = P(s) = \mathbb{E}[R|s]. \tag{27}$$

The objective function is defined as:

$$J(\pi) = \mathbb{E}_{s\sim D}[P(s)], \tag{28}$$

where D is a dataset of observed states and rewards. If actions have partial influence, it is optimized as follows:

$$J(\pi) = \mathbb{E}_{s,a\sim D}[P(s) + A(s,a)]. \tag{29}$$

This formulation bridges RL and supervised learning, enabling RL in non-causal settings, such as:

- Counterfactual reasoning.
- Offline and batch RL.
- Decision-making in complex, non-Markovian environments.

IX. Proposed Training Formulation

In this section, two training algorithms for Heuristic Optimization are proposed: the VQ-VAE model with A3C training and Char-Conv with DQNet-PL, so both character-level and word-level language models are explored.

We define the problem as a Markov Decision Process (MDP) with:

- State space: S
- Action space: A
- Transition dynamics: P
- Reward function: R

The objective is to learn a policy π that maximizes the cumulative expected reward.

A. State Representation

The state at time t, denoted as s_t, represents the environment state:

$$s_t \in S. \tag{30}$$

B. Action Selection

A neural network models the probability distribution for action selection:

$$a_t \sim \pi(a_t|s_t;\theta). \tag{31}$$

The chosen action a_t is sampled from this distribution.

C. Critic Network (Value Estimation)

A critic network estimates the value function $V(s_t)$, representing the expected return from state s_t:

$$V(s_t) = \mathbb{E}\left[\sum_{k=0}^{\infty} \gamma^k r_{t+k}\right]. \tag{32}$$

D. Reward and Return Calculation

The immediate reward r_t is received from the environment. The discounted return is computed as:

$$G_t = r_t + \gamma G_{t+1}. \tag{33}$$

The returns are then normalized:

$$\hat{G}_t = \frac{G_t - \mu}{\sigma + \epsilon}. \tag{34}$$

E. Advantage Estimation

The advantage function measures how much better the taken action was compared to the expected return:

$$A_t = \hat{G}_t - V(s_t). \tag{35}$$

F. Actor-Critic Loss Functions

The loss for the actor (policy gradient) is:

$$L_{\text{actor}} = -\sum_t \log \pi(a_t|s_t) A_t. \tag{36}$$

The critic is updated using the Huber loss:

$$L_{\text{critic}} = \sum_t \text{Huber}(V(s_t), \hat{G}_t). \tag{37}$$

The Huber loss is defined as:

$$\text{Huber}(x, y) = \begin{cases} \frac{1}{2}(x-y)^2, & \text{if } |x-y| < \delta \\ \delta(|x-y| - \frac{1}{2}\delta), & \text{otherwise} \end{cases} \tag{38}$$

G. Gradient Update

The gradients of the total loss function are computed as:

$$\nabla_\theta L_{\text{total}} = \nabla_\theta (L_{\text{actor}} + L_{\text{critic}}). \tag{39}$$

The parameters are updated using the Adam optimizer:

$$\theta \leftarrow \theta - \alpha \nabla_\theta L_{\text{total}}. \tag{40}$$

H. Termination Criteria

Training stops when the running reward exceeds a threshold:

$$\sum_t r_t > R_{\text{target}}. \tag{41}$$

This indicates that the agent has effectively learned an optimal policy for the given task. In this A3C setting, two models are used in order to generate the sequence. In each step a new value and its corresponding position in the sequence (RL state) are generated. Each model has two outputs: one for the action and another for the critic score.

I. Char Conv + DQN-PL

1. Q-Function Approximation

We approximate the action-value function (Q-function) by a neural network with parameters θ:

$$Q(s, a; \theta) \approx \mathbb{E}\left[\sum_{t=0}^{\infty} \gamma^t r_t \,\middle|\, s_0 = s, a_0 = a\right],$$

where:

- s is the state,
- a is the action,
- r_t is the reward at time t,
- γ is the discount factor.

2. Experience Replay

Experiences are stored in a replay buffer as tuples:

$$(s, a, r, s', d),$$

where d is an indicator that equals 1 if s' is terminal and 0 otherwise.

A mini-batch of N experiences is sampled uniformly at random from the replay buffer for training.

3. Target Calculation

For each sampled experience (s, a, r, s', d), the target value y is computed as:

$$y = r + \gamma \max_{a'} Q(s', a'; \theta^-) \cdot (1 - d),$$

where θ^- denotes the parameters of the target network, which are periodically updated to match the primary network parameters θ.

4. Loss Function

The loss function for a mini-batch is defined as the mean squared error between the target and the current Q-value estimate:

$$L(\theta) = \frac{1}{N} \sum_{i=1}^{N} (y_i - Q(s_i, a_i; \theta))^2 .$$

This loss is minimized to update the parameters θ of the Q-network.

5. Gradient Descent Update

The parameters θ are updated via gradient descent:

$$\theta \leftarrow \theta - \alpha \nabla_\theta L(\theta),$$

where α is the learning rate.

6. Action Selection (Epsilon-Greedy Policy)

At each step, the action a is chosen according to the epsilon-greedy strategy:

$$a = \begin{cases} \text{random action}, & \text{with probability } \epsilon, \\ \arg\max_{a'} Q(s, a'; \theta), & \text{with probability } 1 - \epsilon, \end{cases}$$

with ϵ decaying over episodes from an initial value ϵ_{start} to a minimum value ϵ_{min}.

7. Periodic Target Network Update

Every fixed number of episodes (or steps), the target network parameters are updated by copying the weights from the primary network:

$$\theta^- \leftarrow \theta$$

X. Accessed Problems

For each of the two described ways to generate sequences, causal or non-causal, and regarding the Reinforcement Learning (RL) usage along with the proposed architectures, one benchmark problem was selected. The Traveling Salesman Problem (TSP) for causal generation and Neural Architecture Search (NAS) for non-causal generation.

A. Traveling Salesman Problem

The TSP consists of generating a tour from a given starting city that passes through all the other cities while minimizing the overall path distance. The considered cities have the following coordinates:

TABLE I. CITIES' COORDINATES USED IN THE TRAVELING SALESMAN PROBLEM.

X	Y
23	45
57	12
38	78
92	34
45	67
18	90
72	55
66	24
83	62
49	40

A distance matrix is calculated based on the euclidean distance between all the cities. A boolean array is used to track the cities already visited. If a generated city is already visited, the reward function gets the value of -100, in contrary, if a city is not visited, then the reward function gets the value given by:

$$\text{normalized\_reward} = 100 \cdot \left(1 - \frac{\text{distance}}{\text{max\_distance}}\right)$$

With:

$$\text{distance} = \text{distance\_matrix}[\text{current\_city}][\text{action}]$$

The cities road is generated iteratively, one city after another until the generated city is already visited. When this final condition is met, the obtained road is evaluated and the current episode ends.

B. Neural Architecture Search

For the NAS problem, the sequence is interpreted as the Network Structure Code (NSC), meaning that it encodes an Artificial Neural Network (ANN). In this case, it is intended to generate a neural text classifier architecture built by several InceptionV1 blocks [56]. The NSC is composed by two decoupled models which contribute to the same RL final state, also known as NSC. The reward function is the child-network training accuracy which, in the current problem's case, is a classifier network. This classifier is built from an inverted n-ary tree encoded in Depth-First-Search (DFS).

XI. RESULTS

In this section, the performance plots for the NAS problem are presented. The adopted search space is an encoded n-ary tree using Depth First Search (DFS). The tree is encoded using $[0, 1, 2]$ in a sequence with a maximum of five positions. A zero encodes a change in the tree branch, a one encodes a deeper instruction, and the two is interpreted as a padding character. Each tree element is a Conv1D version of an InceptionV1 block [56]. When constructed, the tree is inverted so that the root node represents the classifier's final decision kernel. The search focuses on a text classifier, where the embeddings are provided by a Keras embedding layer. For evaluation purposes, this layer is replaced by the RoBERTa large model from Hugging Face [57], achieving state-of-the-art results with the IMDB sentiment analysis dataset [58]. The resulting model from the search was trained using a learning rate scheduler and presents the training curves shown in Figure 3.

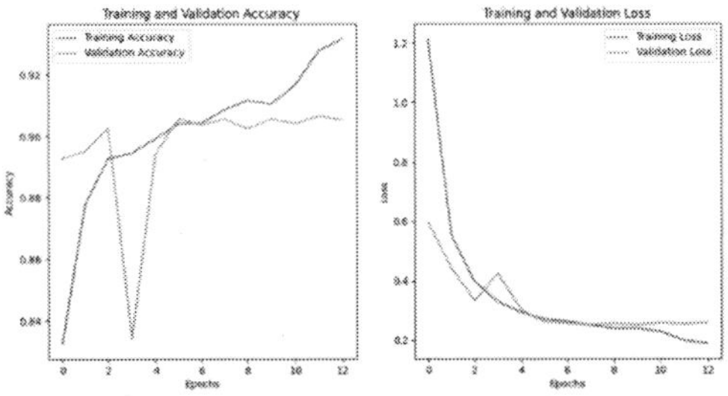

Figure 3. Classification accuracy and binary cross-entropy loss when using the generated NAS classifier and RoBERTa as embedding model.

The resulting binary text classifier positioning in the state of the art is presented in Table III.

TABLE II. FINAL MODEL RESULTS ON IMDB SENTIMENT ANALYSIS DATASET.

Test Loss	0.25214493327468872
Test Accuracy	0.90548974275558899

The results presented were obtained by replacing the embedding layer with a pre-trained model from [59].

TABLE III. IMDB SENTIMENT ANALYSIS TEST SET ACCURACY FOR DIFFERENT MODELS IN THE LITERATURE

Model	Accuracy (%)	Reference
Naive Bayes (Baseline)	83.5	[60]
LSTM (Long Short-Term Memory)	89.0	[61]
BiLSTM with Attention	91.2	[62]
FastText	88.5	[63]
RoBERTa+NAS Tree-based Classifier	90.5	-
CNN (Convolutional Networks)	90.6	[64]
ULMFiT (Pretrained LSTM)	94.0	[65]
BERT-base (Fine-tuned)	95.2	[66]
RoBERTa (Fine-tuned)	96.3	[67]
DistilBERT	95.1	[68]
GPT-2 (Fine-tuned)	95.0	[69]
XLNet	96.4	[70]
ALBERT	95.8	[71]
ELECTRA	96.6	[72]
T5 (Text-to-Text Transfer)	96.1	[73]
GPT-3 (Few-shot)	94.7	[74]
DeBERTa (Fine-tuned)	96.7	[75]
ChatGPT (Prompting)	96.0*	[76]

The neural architecture search task was performed using both language models: character-level using SoftQLearning and word-level using asynchronous advantage actor-critic training. In both cases, the problem's probability density function for each output was predicted by the models, and the final output is a result of a random experience with the model-predicted odds. This feature allows the models to represent more complex problems, such as NAS. This behavior also enables the model to learn the probabilistic aspects of a dataset; by fixing a serializable data ontology, it can generate datasets. Returning to the scope of this article, more specifically regarding these models' optimization capability in the NAS task, the learning and performance curves are presented below.

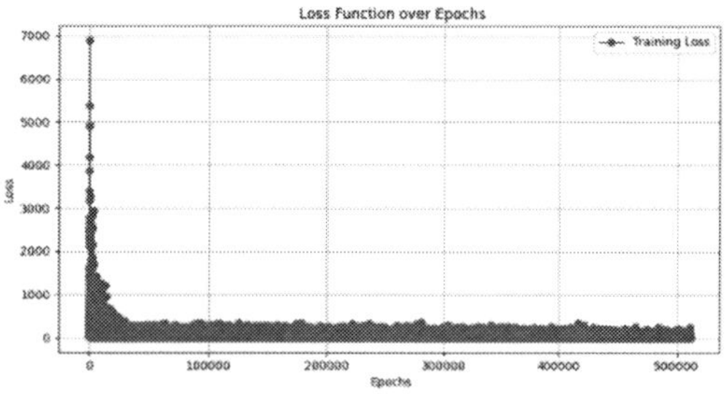

Figure 4. Loss function of SoftQ-Leaning using Char-Conv inspired architecture.

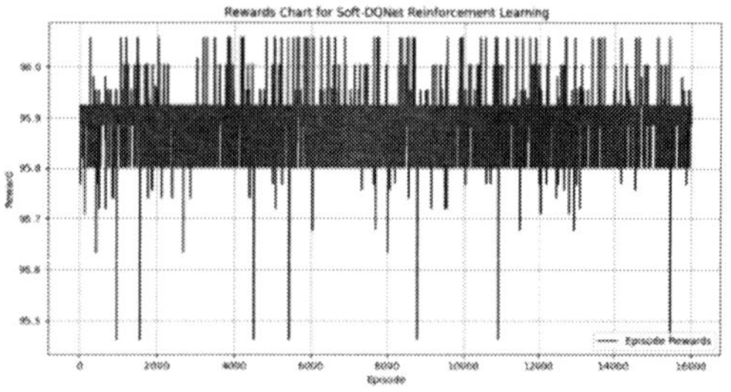

Figure 5. RL reward function, child network's training accuracy, using SoftQ-Leaning using Char-Conv inspired architecture.

In the above experiment the model presented in [48], has two decoupled outputs which are used to compose the sequence - Network Structure Code. The Soft Q-Learning training method was adopted instead of DQNet-PL because the latest presents a very high training variance, making the training to not converge. Additionally the entropy regularization also helped to attain training convergence.

The transformer-based Vector Quantized Variational Auto Encoder (VQ-VAE) follows the same decoupling logic to compose the sequence, as described previously. In this case, the model has two outputs: the actor and the critic. The actor predicts odds for each possible model action, and the second output, the critic rates the overall model performance. In terms of architecture, the actor-critic decoupling is made only in the model's last layer to shape the output according to the needs to generate the critic score and actor's odds.

Two Transformer-based VQ-VAE models were used to compose the sequence, one to generate the action and another to generate the position in the candidate sequence where the action value will be assigned. Bellow, the obtained training curves are presented:

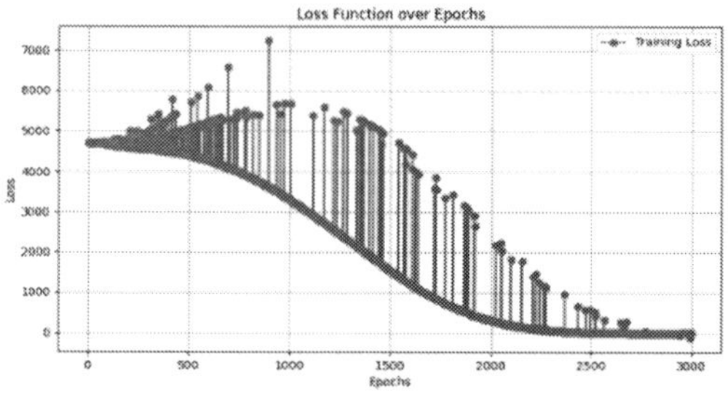

Figure 6. Loss function of action sequence composing parameter during the A3C training using Transformer inspired architecture.

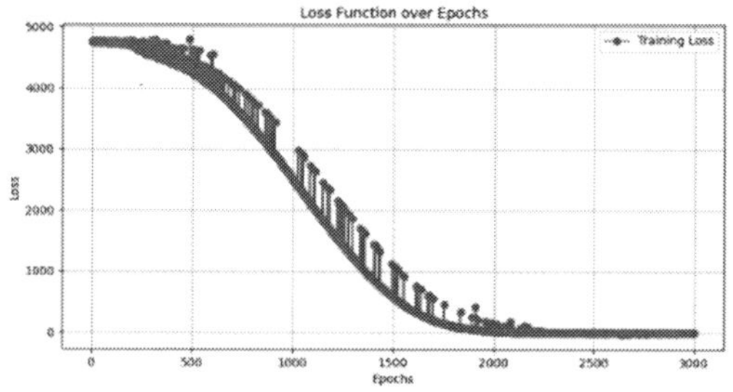

Figure 7. Position loss function of A3C using Transformer inspired architecture.

The observable outliers are due to the epsilon-greedy technique used to introduce exploration in the algorithm's behavior. All the loss function plots in the presented results converge to zero, and the reward signals reflect the overfitting tendency of the proposed NAS methodology. The decoupling strategies are effective in stabilizing the training methodologies in both character and word-level approaches. Additionally, the sequence generalization and problem modeling capabilities are

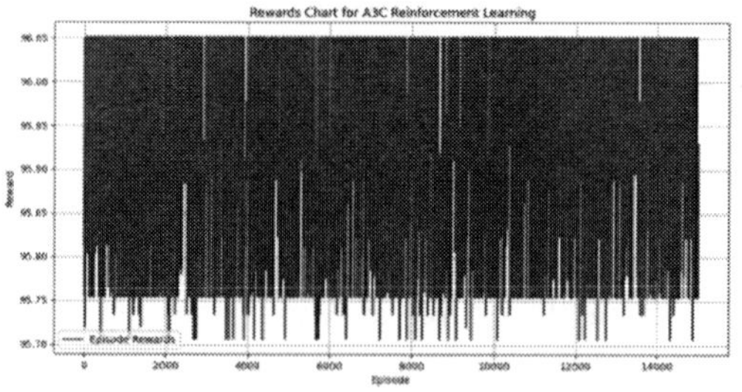

Figure 8. RL reward and child network accuracy as functions of A3C using a Transformer-inspired architecture.

verified when observing the obtained training curves; both approaches exhibit stable behavior.

Next, the Traveling Salesman Problem results are presented. Experiments with both the architectures are presented bellow.

Starting from the Char-Conv as DQNet and as well as Policy network, the results were the following:

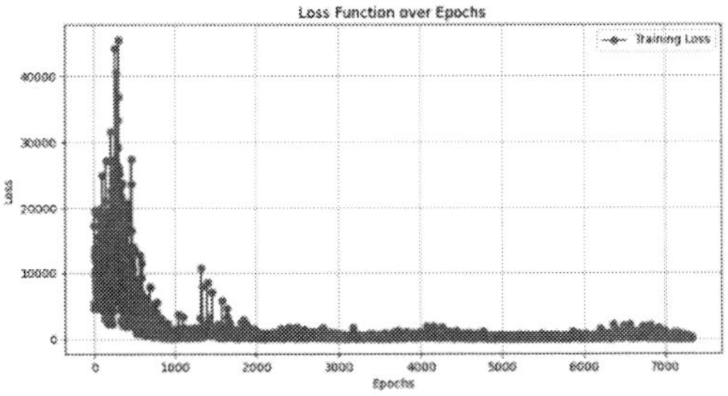

Figure 9. Char-Conv architecture's loss function during the DQNet-PL training, while solving the Traveling Salesman problem.

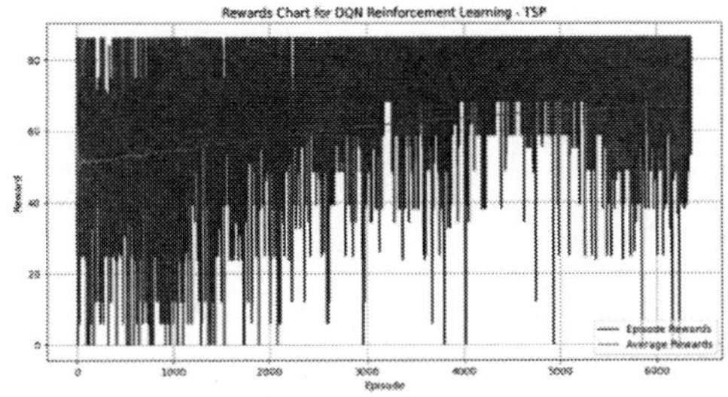

Figure 10. Reward function of Char-Conv architecture during the DQNet-PL training, while solving the TSP problem.

Both curves indicate that the RL agent is learning, as evidenced by the loss function's convergence to zero and the reward function's increasing behavior during training. Next, the VQ-VAE model is used in conjunction with A3C training to generate the salesman route:

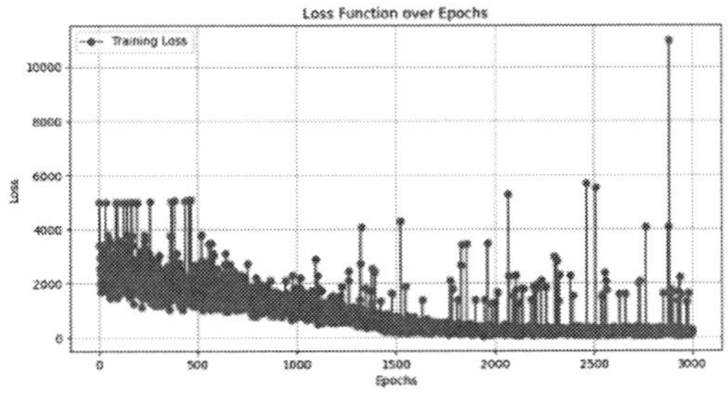

Figure 11. Loss function during the A3C training using Transformer inspired architecture in the TSP problem resolution.

The loss function chart exhibits zero convergence; therefore, training stability is concluded, and the generally increasing reward function reflects the VQ-VAE agent's learning. Depending on the problem complexity, generating action odds might

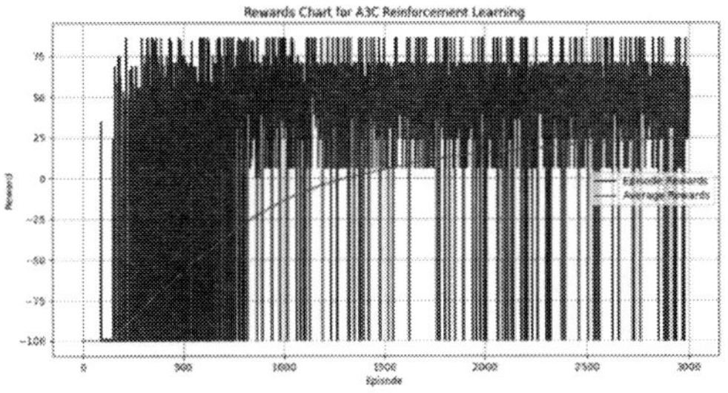

Figure 12. Reward function obtained by the VQ-VAE based agent in A3C.

be preferred rather than generating the agent's actions directly, as occurred with the Char-Conv architecture in NAS, where Soft-Q Learning was used, and in the TSP where DQNet-PL was utilized. The Transformer-inspired VQ-VAE demonstrates overall better training behavior compared to the Char-Conv architecture, as this model can map the search space into several sub-regions by utilizing the Vector-Quantized layer, thereby parallelizing the search.

XII. Error Analysis

During the experimentation phase of this work, the Traveling Salesman benchmark problem was addressed using A3C training together with the Transformer-based VQ-VAE model. Additionally, the Char-Conv model was tested alongside DQNet-PL training on the same problem. After several unsuccessful experiments resulted from the usual issues of high variance in the reward signal and a non-converging loss function, a functional decoupling methodology was developed and successfully applied to the TSP problem. The training results are presented in Figures 9 and 11 for the Char-Conv and VQ-VAE models, respectively.

In considering the NAS problem, the combination of Char-Conv with DQN-PL training did not succeed in solving this issue, as the loss function did not converge to zero. In contrast, the combination of VQ-VAE, A3C, and the respective decoupling effectively solved the problem (Figures 6 and 7). To address the limitations of solving the NAS problem using CharConv, SoftQ Learning with entropy regulation was employed, as it enables modeling the odds of each output and reduces the variance of the reward signal.

XIII. Conclusions and Future Work

Many problems are non-sequential and do not require strict left-to-right order dependency. To handle such cases, a value-position decoupling strategy is proposed. Considering the Transformer-based VQ-VAE trained with A3C, the model has two outputs: an actor output and a critic output. Instead of using two models, a single model is employed. In this way, the network weights are updated on both occasions: when the actor learns and when the critic learns. Two A3C models with a shared state and reward are used; one generates the new element's position, and the other generates the new element's values. The VQ-VAE architecture has the capability to divide the latent space into quantized subspaces and perform a parallelized search in each subspace.

The deep convolutional network, which is trained using Deep Q-Learning for value generation and Soft Q-Learning for sequence generation, applies similar reasoning to design the training. One model with two outputs is responsible for generating the new element's position, while another model generates the new element's value. To make this training generative, the output odds are modeled, and the outputs are generated using a random experiment in which each output odd is defined by the Deep Q-models. Additionally, to reduce training variance, an entropy term is added to the loss function. This process is called entropy regularization and promotes training convergence towards zero.

This study demonstrates that it is possible to generate sequences without causality constraints while still using slightly adapted Reinforcement Learning techniques. Training convergence is improved if the same model with two outputs is used to perform actions and to critique its performance, regardless of its architecture. In both cases, Transformer and Char-Conv, it was the most performant architectural variation and performed heuristic search in this manner. Complex ontologies describing the candidate solutions can be encoded and serialized into integer sequences. The encoded sequences can then be optimized by this type of solver when used together with a performance metric designed as the Reinforcement Learning reward. Since sufficient decoupling is achieved, the language models can absorb the problem's semantics and generate admissible candidate solutions of increasing quality. The position-value decoupling must be employed in the NAS scenario to avoid imposing causality in the sequence generation during the RL training. Additionally, using variational models in complex RL environments such as NAS is more efficient since they model the environment's unknown properties. The Transformer-based VQ-VAE is also capable of parallelizing the search due to the vector quantization layer.

Looking toward the future, the models presented, along with the proposed training techniques, can be used to generate more than encoded solutions for a given problem. By selecting an appropriate reward function, the generated sequence can be utilized in the standard format to produce content, similar to Generative Adversarial Networks.

A comparison of the proposed solvers, together with other state-of-the-art heuristic search algorithms, can be made to systematically explore the limitations of this proposal and extend its applicability domain. An analysis of the problem's degrees of freedom versus processing time will be conducted, focusing on solver quality analysis based on degrees of freedom, the solver's scaling with DoF, and the algorithm's parallelization.

References

[1] D. P. Kingma and M. Welling, "Auto-encoding variational bayes," *arXiv preprint arXiv:1312.6114*, 2013.

[2] D. J. Rezende, S. Mohamed, and D. Wierstra, "Stochastic backpropagation and approximate inference in deep generative models," *arXiv preprint arXiv:1401.4082*, 2014.

[3] I. Higgins *et al.*, "Beta-vae: Learning basic visual concepts with a constrained variational framework," in *International Conference on Learning Representations*, 2017.

[4] D. P. Kingma, S. Mohamed, D. J. Rezende, and M. Welling, "Semi-supervised learning with deep generative models," in *Advances in Neural Information Processing Systems*, 2014, pp. 3581–3589.

[5] C. P. Burgess *et al.*, "Understanding disentangling in beta-vae," *arXiv preprint arXiv:1804.03599*, 2018.

[6] K. Sohn, H. Lee, and X. Yan, "Learning structured output representation using deep conditional generative models," in *Advances in Neural Information Processing Systems*, 2015, pp. 3483–3491.

[7] X. Chen *et al.*, "Infogan: Interpretable representation learning by information maximizing generative adversarial nets," *arXiv preprint arXiv:1606.03657*, 2016.

[8] C. Doersch, "Tutorial on variational autoencoders," *arXiv preprint arXiv:1606.05908*, 2016.

[9] D. J. Rezende and S. Mohamed, "Variational inference with normalizing flows," *arXiv preprint arXiv:1505.05770*, 2015.

[10] N. Dilokthanakul *et al.*, "Deep unsupervised clustering with gaussian mixture variational autoencoders," *arXiv preprint arXiv:1611.02648*, 2016.

[11] I. Tolstikhin, O. Bousquet, S. Gelly, and B. Schölkopf, "Wasserstein auto-encoders," *arXiv preprint arXiv:1711.01558*, 2017.

[12] I. Goodfellow *et al.*, "Generative adversarial nets," in *Advances in Neural Information Processing Systems*, 2014, pp. 2672–2680.

[13] A. Radford, L. Metz, and S. Chintala, "Unsupervised representation learning with deep convolutional generative adversarial networks," in *International Conference on Learning Representations*, 2016.

[14] M. Arjovsky, S. Chintala, and L. Bottou, "Wasserstein gan," *arXiv preprint arXiv:1701.07875*, 2017.

[15] I. Gulrajani, F. Ahmed, M. Arjovsky, V. Dumoulin, and A. C. Courville, "Improved training of wasserstein gans," in *Advances in Neural Information Processing Systems*, 2017, pp. 5767–5777.

[16] T. Karras, S. Laine, and T. Aila, "A style-based generator architecture for generative adversarial networks," in *Proceedings of the IEEE Conference on Computer Vision and Pattern Recognition*, 2019, pp. 4401–4410.

[17] A. Brock, J. Donahue, and K. Simonyan, "Large scale gan training for high fidelity natural image synthesis," *arXiv preprint arXiv:1809.11096*, 2018.

[18] A. Creswell *et al.*, "Generative adversarial networks: An overview," *IEEE Signal Processing Magazine*, vol. 35, no. 1, pp. 53–65, 2018.

[19] H. Ishfaq, A. Hoogi, and D. Rubin, "TVAE: Triplet-Based Variational Autoencoder using Metric Learning," no. 2015, pp. 1–4, 2018. arXiv: 1802.04403.

[20] S. Paul, *Vector-Quantized Variational Autoencoders*, 2021.

[21] J. H. Holland, *Adaptation in Natural and Artificial Systems: An Introductory Analysis with Applications to Biology, Control, and Artificial Intelligence*. University of Michigan Press, 1975.

[22] D. E. Goldberg, "Genetic algorithms in search, optimization, and machine learning," in *Addison-Wesley*, 1989.

[23] K. A. De Jong, "An analysis of the behavior of a class of genetic adaptive systems," *Doctoral dissertation, University of Michigan*, 1975.

[24] J. H. Holland, "Building blocks, fringe search, and genetic algorithms," in *Foundations of Genetic Algorithms*, vol. 1, 1992, pp. 1–8.

[25] M. Mitchell, "An introduction to genetic algorithms," *MIT Press*, 1996.

[26] J. R. Koza, "Genetic programming: On the programming of computers by means of natural selection," in *MIT Press*, 1992.
[27] D. Whitley, "A genetic algorithm tutorial," *Statistics and Computing*, vol. 4, no. 2, pp. 65–85, 1994.
[28] D. E. Goldberg and K. Deb, "Comparative analysis of selection schemes used in genetic algorithms," *Foundations of Genetic Algorithms*, vol. 1, pp. 69–93, 1991.
[29] K. Deb, "Multi-objective optimization using evolutionary algorithms," *Wiley*, 2001.
[30] T. Bäck, "Evolutionary algorithms in theory and practice: Evolution strategies, evolutionary programming, genetic algorithms," *Oxford University Press*, 1996.
[31] Y. Bengio, R. Ducharme, P. Vincent, and C. Janvin, "A neural probabilistic language model," *Journal of Machine Learning Research*, vol. 3, pp. 1137–1155, 2003.
[32] J. L. Elman, "Finding structure in time," in *Cognitive Science*, vol. 14, 1990, pp. 179–211.
[33] S. Hochreiter and J. Schmidhuber, "Long short-term memory," *Neural Computation*, vol. 9, no. 8, pp. 1735–1780, 1997.
[34] A. Radford, K. Narasimhan, T. Salimans, and I. Sutskever, "Improving language understanding by generative pre-training," *OpenAI preprint*, 2018.
[35] J. Devlin, M.-W. Chang, K. Lee, and K. Toutanova, "Bert: Pre-training of deep bidirectional transformers for language understanding," *arXiv preprint arXiv:1810.04805*, 2018.
[36] D. Bahdanau, K. Cho, and Y. Bengio, "Neural machine translation by jointly learning to align and translate," *arXiv preprint arXiv:1409.0473*, 2014.
[37] Y. Goldberg, "A primer on neural network models for natural language processing," *Journal of Artificial Intelligence Research*, vol. 57, pp. 345–420, 2016.
[38] T. Young, D. Hazarika, S. Poria, and E. Cambria, "Recent trends in deep learning based natural language processing," *IEEE Computational Intelligence Magazine*, vol. 13, no. 3, pp. 55–75, 2018.
[39] I. Sutskever, O. Vinyals, and Q. V. Le, "Sequence to sequence learning with neural networks," *Advances in Neural Information Processing Systems*, pp. 3104–3112, 2014.
[40] K. Cho *et al.*, "Learning phrase representations using rnn encoder-decoder for statistical machine translation," in *Proceedings of the 2014 Conference on Empirical Methods in Natural Language Processing (EMNLP)*, 2014, pp. 1724–1734.
[41] M.-T. Luong, H. Pham, and C. D. Manning, "Effective approaches to attention-based neural machine translation," *arXiv preprint arXiv:1508.04025*, 2015.
[42] Y. Wu *et al.*, "Google's neural machine translation system: Bridging the gap between human and machine translation," *arXiv preprint arXiv:1609.08144*, 2016.
[43] M. Johnson *et al.*, "Google's multilingual neural machine translation system: Enabling zero-shot translation," *Transactions of the Association for Computational Linguistics*, vol. 5, pp. 339–351, 2017.
[44] C. Chu, R. Wang, and R. Dabre, "A survey of domain adaptation for neural machine translation," *arXiv preprint arXiv:1806.00258*, 2018.
[45] B. Zoph and Q. V. Le, "Neural architecture search with reinforcement learning," *5th International Conference on Learning Representations, ICLR 2017 - Conference Track Proceedings*, pp. 1–16, 2017. arXiv: 1611.01578.
[46] C. Liu *et al.*, "Progressive Neural Architecture Search," in *Lecture Notes in Computer Science (including subseries Lecture Notes in Artificial Intelligence and Lecture Notes in Bioinformatics)*, vol. 11205 LNCS, 2017, pp. 19–35, ISBN: 9783030012458. DOI: 10.1007/978-3-030-01246-5_2. arXiv: 1712.00559.
[47] T. Shen *et al.*, "Minimum risk training for neural machine translation," in *Proceedings of the 54th Annual Meeting of the Association for Computational Linguistics (ACL)*, 2016, pp. 1689–1699.
[48] X. Zhang and Y. LeCun, "Text Understanding from Scratch," 2015. arXiv: 1502.01710.
[49] A. Vaswani *et al.*, "Attention is all you need," *Advances in Neural Information Processing Systems*, vol. 2017-December, no. Nips, pp. 5999–6009, 2017, ISSN: 10495258. arXiv: 1706.03762.
[50] V. Mnih *et al.*, "Human-level control through deep reinforcement learning," *Nature*, vol. 518, no. 7540, pp. 529–533, 2015.
[51] T. Schaul, J. Quan, I. Antonoglou, and D. Silver, "Prioritized experience replay," in *International Conference on Learning Representations (ICLR)*, 2016.
[52] V. Mnih *et al.*, "Asynchronous methods for deep reinforcement learning," in *International Conference on Machine Learning (ICML)*, PMLR, 2016, pp. 1928–1937.
[53] T. Haarnoja, H. Tang, P. Abbeel, and S. Levine, "Reinforcement learning with deep energy-based policies," in *International Conference on Machine Learning (ICML)*, PMLR, 2017, pp. 1352–1361.
[54] OpenAI, *Chatgpt response to a question about citing chatgpt in ieee format*, https://chatgpt.com/share/67f049a9-44a4-800b-af33-64211def3a0b, Accessed: Apr. 4, 2025, 2025.
[55] OpenAI, *Chatgpt response to a request for a .bib representation of a shared conversation*, https://chatgpt.com/share/67f04ae1-7590-800b-8e4d-72623a1801dc, Accessed: Apr. 4, 2025, 2025.
[56] C. Szegedy, S. Reed, P. Sermanet, V. Vanhoucke, and A. Rabinovich, "Going deeper with convolutions," pp. 1–12, arXiv: arXiv:1409.4842v1.
[57] Y. Liu *et al.*, "Roberta: A robustly optimized BERT pretraining approach," *CoRR*, vol. abs/1907.11692, 2019. arXiv: 1907.11692.
[58] S. Tripathi, R. Mehrotra, V. Bansal, and S. Upadhyay, "Analyzing sentiment using imdb dataset," in *2020 12th International Conference on Computational Intelligence and Communication Networks (CICN)*, 2020, pp. 30–33. DOI: 10.1109/CICN49253.2020.9242570.
[59] A. L. Maas *et al.*, "Learning word vectors for sentiment analysis," in *Proceedings of the 49th Annual Meeting of the Association for Computational Linguistics: Human Language Technologies*, Portland, Oregon, USA: Association for Computational Linguistics, 2011, pp. 142–150.
[60] B. Pang and L. Lee, "Thumbs up? sentiment classification using machine learning techniques," in *Proceedings of the ACL*, Association for Computational Linguistics, 2002.
[61] D. Tang, B. Qin, and T. Liu, "Document modeling with gated recurrent neural network for sentiment classification," in *Proceedings of the 2015 conference on empirical methods in natural language processing (EMNLP)*, 2015, pp. 1422–1432.
[62] P. Zhou *et al.*, "Attention-based bidirectional long short-term memory networks for relation classification," *Proceedings of ACL*, 2016.
[63] A. Joulin, E. Grave, P. Bojanowski, and T. Mikolov, "Bag of tricks for efficient text classification," in *Proceedings of the 15th Conference of the European Chapter of the Association for Computational Linguistics: Volume 2, Short Papers*, vol. 2, 2017, pp. 427–431.
[64] R. Johnson and T. Zhang, "Deep pyramid convolutional neural networks for text categorization," *ACL*, 2017.
[65] J. Howard and S. Ruder, "Universal language model fine-tuning for text classification," in *Proceedings of the 56th Annual Meeting of the Association for Computational Linguistics (Volume 1: Long Papers)*, 2018, pp. 328–339.
[66] J. Devlin, M.-W. Chang, K. Lee, and K. Toutanova, "Bert: Pre-training of deep bidirectional transformers for language understanding," in *Proceedings of the 2019 Conference of the*

North American Chapter of the Association for Computational Linguistics: Human Language Technologies, 2019.
[67] Y. Liu *et al.*, "Roberta: A robustly optimized bert pretraining approach," *arXiv preprint arXiv:1907.11692*, 2019.
[68] V. Sanh, L. Debut, J. Chaumond, and T. Wolf, "Distilbert, a distilled version of bert: Smaller, faster, cheaper and lighter," *arXiv preprint arXiv:1910.01108*, 2020.
[69] A. Radford *et al.*, "Language models are unsupervised multitask learners," *OpenAI blog*, vol. 1, no. 8, 2019.
[70] Z. Yang *et al.*, "Xlnet: Generalized autoregressive pretraining for language understanding," in *Proceedings of the 33rd International Conference on Neural Information Processing Systems*, 2019.
[71] Z. Lan *et al.*, "Albert: A lite bert for self-supervised learning of language representations," *arXiv preprint arXiv:1909.11942*, 2020.
[72] K. Clark, M.-T. Luong, Q. V. Le, and C. D. Manning, "Electra: Pre-training text encoders as discriminators rather than generators," in *ICLR*, 2020.
[73] C. Raffel *et al.*, "Exploring the limits of transfer learning with a unified text-to-text transformer," *JMLR*, 2020.
[74] T. B. Brown *et al.*, "Language models are few-shot learners," in *Advances in Neural Information Processing Systems*, vol. 33, 2020, pp. 1877–1901.
[75] P. He, X. Liu, J. Gao, and W. Chen, "Deberta: Decoding-enhanced bert with disentangled attention," *ICLR*, 2021.
[76] OpenAI, "Gpt-4 technical report," *OpenAI Technical Reports*, 2023.

Optimizing Resource Management in Algerian Traditional Brick Manufacturing (SNG) Using Blockchain-Based Smart Contracts with Solidity

Aimene Boughrira, Samia Aitouche, El Hocine Grabsi, Hichem Aouag, Kamel Taouririt, Khireddine Bourmel
Laboratory of Automation and Manufacturing (LAP), Batna 2 University
Batna, Algeria
E-mail: aimene.boughrira@univ-batna2.dz, s.aitouche@univ-batna2.dz, elhocine.grabsi@etu.univ-batna2.dz, h.aouag@univ-batna2.dz, taouriritkamel@hotmail.fr, khireddine.bourmel@etu.univ-batna2.dz

Abstract—**Resource management is the strategic process of efficiently planning, organizing and controlling resources, such as: time, money, materials and personnel to achieve organizational goals. Different crucial roles are played by it, such as waste minimization, cost reduction, time protection, energy conservation, and productivity enhancement, while sustainability and adaptability in dynamic environments are ensured. In summary, it is a process regarded as essential for the achievement of long-term success. In addition, optimizing resource management is a critical challenge across all fields, particularly in the industrial sector, where inefficiencies lead to negative impacts. Effective strategies require balancing resource allocation, energy consumption and production output while maintaining sustainability. Advances in technology, such as Artificial Intelligence (AI), Internet of Things (IoT) and blockchain offer promising solutions to enhance efficiency and revolutionize the whole of the industrial field. In our study, we discuss the implementation and local adaptation of a Blockchain-driven inventory and production management solution, based on a smart contract model that is already operational in other countries but not yet adopted in Algeria (Batna) uniquely tailored for a traditional brick manufacturing industry. Modular Smart Contracts will form part of this system (where challenges like inefficiencies, lack of trust, waste, and high costs persist), enabling a number of operational needs-from the raw material management, production oversight, to inventory administration. These Smart Contracts of integration in the study measure how Blockchain can enhance transparency, efficiency, and reliability in managing the resources at different stages of the brick production process.**

Keywords- Optimization; Blockchain; Smart contracts; Resource management.

I. INTRODUCTION

The manufacturing industry is a cornerstone of global economies, driving innovation, creating jobs and supporting economic growth through the production of goods using labor, machinery and advanced technology [1]. Resource management [2] [3] plays a crucial role in the industrial sector, ensuring optimal use of materials, energy, and labor while reducing costs and environmental impact [4]. However, traditional industrial systems face numerous challenges, including inefficiencies in resource allocation and reliance on manual processes that are error-prone and time-consuming, leading to waste and increased costs. Limited integration between departments or supply chain stages creates communication gaps and operational silos, while dependence on intermediaries and centralized control increases risks, delays, and downtime. These systems also lack transparency, making it difficult to monitor operations effectively and ensure data security. Furthermore, outdated infrastructure struggles to scale or adapt to changing market demands or technological advancements, hampering growth and competitiveness. High operational costs and environmental inefficiencies further hinder efforts to achieve sustainability and long-term success. Since its emergence in 2008 [5], blockchain technology has provided effective scientific proposals, some of which have been implemented on the ground and some of which are still under development. Moreover, reliance on Smart Contracts has led to offer innovative solutions by enabling secure, decentralized and automated processes that address these limitations [6].

This paper focuses on developing a blockchain-based system for a brick factory, demonstrating how Smart Contracts can streamline operations, enhance resource utilization and transform industrial practices for greater efficiency and transparency. It is organized as follows: Section 2 offers an overview about the appearance of Blockchain and Smart Contracts in the scientific field and its applications in Inventory Management (IM). Section 3 describes the need for Smart Contracts for brick factories and its key features. Section 4 gives us a case study in an Algerian factory named New General Society "SNG". Results and discussions appear in Section 6. The final section presents the conclusion and future work.

II. LITERATURE REVIEW

A. Overview of Blockchain and Smart Contracts

The fast advancement of technology has resulted in revolutionary developments, altering industries and reinventing how people communicate [7], trade, and trust in a digital environment. Among these innovations, Blockchain technology and Smart Contracts stand out as game-changing tools that offer unprecedented security, transparency, and efficiency in modern processes. Blockchain, often known as the backbone of digital trust, provides a decentralized and immutable framework for recording transactions and managing data. Its distributed structure eliminates the need for middlemen [8], resulting in a system that prioritizes transparency and security. In addition, Smart Contracts, which are self-executing agreements [9] inscribed directly on the blockchain, add a layer of automation that simplifies procedures, reduces costs, and maintains reliability.

This section investigates the foundations of Blockchain and Smart Contracts, including their essential characteristics, applications and synergies when combined. Understanding these technologies enables us to address long-standing difficulties in areas such as supply chain management, banking, healthcare, and so on. This preamble serves as an introduction to a world where technology promotes trust, efficiency and creativity, paving the path for a more linked and safe future.

We began browsing for literature relating to Blockchain and Smart Contracts and data was acquired from the Scopus and Google Scholar databases. We looked at just scientific publications published in English since 2024. After the screening step, we rated irrelevant publications based on duplication, title, abstract substance, etc. To choose the target objects, we were quite careful about several key features. Table I outlines the main key features of Blockchain (BC) and Smart Contracts (SC).

TABLE I. SAMPLE OF KEY FEATURES OF BC AND SC.

Aspect / Key Features	Blockchain	Smart Contracts
Decentralization	Data is shared across multiple nodes, removing reliance on a central authority [10].	Operates on decentralized networks, ensuring independence from central intermediaries [15].
Immutability	Data cannot be altered or deleted once recorded, ensuring a tamper-proof system [11].	Contract terms and conditions cannot be modified after deployment, ensuring integrity [16].
Transparency	Transactions and data are visible to authorized participants, fostering trust [12].	Contract terms are accessible to all authorized participants, enhancing transparency [17].
Security	Cryptographic techniques and consensus protocols protect data from unauthorized access [13].	Transactions and conditions are securely validated within the blockchain environment [18].
Automation	Enables the use of Smart Contracts for self-executing processes [14].	Automatically executes predefined actions when conditions are met, reducing manual intervention [18].
Cost Efficiency	Reduces intermediaries, lowering operational and transaction costs [8] [16].	Minimizes the need for third-party involvement, cutting down costs associated with execution [18][19].

B. Applications of Blockchain in Inventory Management

Inventory Management (IM) covers a wide range of fields that ensure efficient control, tracking, and distribution of goods within an organization. Table II summarizes some fields of Inventory Management and their potential relationship with Blockchain (BC).

TABLE II. RELATIONSHIP BETWEEN IM AND BC.

Field of IM	Blockchain footprint
Stock Control	Improves transparency and accuracy in stock levels by providing real-time transaction updates and reducing human errors or discrepancies in inventory data [20].
Inventory Tracking	Enables secure, real-time tracking of goods from suppliers to customers, enhancing accuracy and reducing fraud or tampering [21].
Supply Chain Management	Provides a transparent, auditable, and immutable record of all transactions in the supply chain, enhancing traceability, efficiency, and reducing delays or fraud [22].
Order Management	Streamlines order management by recording and verifying every step, ensuring accuracy and reducing disputes between suppliers, distributors, and customers [23].
Demand Forecasting	Provides transparent historical sales data and transactions, enabling the prediction of future inventory needs [24].
Warehouse Management	Enhances warehouse management efficiency by providing a comprehensive record of goods movements, improving operations, and reducing human error [25].
Inventory Replenishment	Smart Contracts automate inventory replenishment by triggering reorders when stock thresholds are met, ensuring timely restocking without human intervention [23].
Stock Auditing and Reconciliation	Ensures that inventory data is unaltered, facilitating audits and reconciling discrepancies between physical inventory and system records [26].
Returns and Reverse Logistics	Records the history of returned items, ensuring their proper processing, tracking, and potential re-entry into inventory, while minimizing fraudulent returns [27].
Risk Management	Enhances supply chain resilience by providing transparent records and mitigating risk through smart contract automation [28].

C. Research Gaps

Our analysis highlights a significant gap in the existing research on traditional brick factories in our region, largely due to the limited adoption of emerging technologies that could improve traceability and transparency. To address this gap, a comprehensive examination of the specific challenges and opportunities within this manufacturing sector is necessary. Furthermore, incorporating innovative concepts, such as Blockchain technology and Smart Contracts could pave the way for new solutions designed to reduce energy consumption, enhance the traceability, transparency, sustainability of brick IM.

III. Methodology and Case Study

A. Description

SNG (Société Nouvelle Générale) is a private company founded by the Spanish firm Equipceramic in 2013. However, in 2019, a number of socio-political events took place. The facility was nationalized from private ownership in order to support the growth of Batna, Algeria's building materials sector. The company specializes in manufacturing and delivering construction materials. On the ground at the factory site, such change in developments did not cease production and sales. This plant went into a public auction in April 2024. Currently, SNG has 135 employees working in a variety of departments and services, all of whom are under general management. The location of the factory between 3 provinces (Batna, Setif, and Khenchla) puts it in a strategic position to take advantage when it comes to logistics and distribution. The factory is divided into three zones with an area of 75,000 m² each (Raw Material Park, Manufacturing Workshop, Equipment and Spare Parts Warehouse, and Finished Product Storage). The continuity of SNG's operational ability despite ownership changes proves its vital role in Batna's industrial ecosystem. The factory has a daily production capacity of around 10,000 bricks; this is positive potential to integrate our Smart Contracts.

B. Manufacturing Process

Brick production involves several key stages, as illustrated in Figure 1.

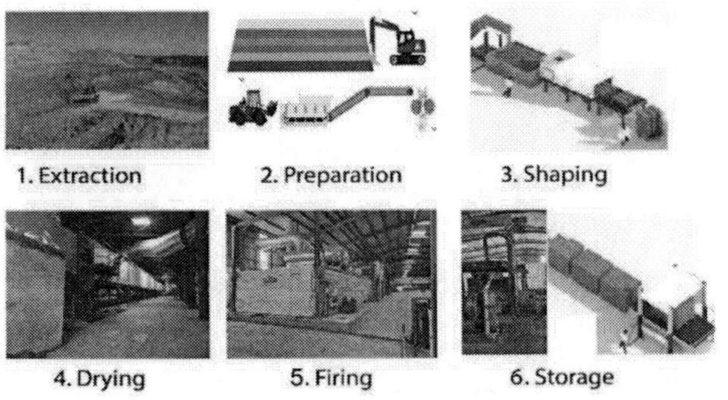

Figure 1. Manufacturing Process of SNG.

1. Extraction: Mechanically extract clay from the ground to deliver it to the park.
2. Preparation: The raw clay is homogenized by crushing, mixing, refining, and moistening.
3. Shaping: To get the required characteristic textures materials (mixture of clay, sand and water) and formed into bricks.
4. Drying: To ensure sufficient strength for stacking and burning, the bricks are dried under regulated conditions, bringing the moisture content down to around 2%.
5. Firing: The bricks are fired in a tunnel kiln, where the bricks go through physical and chemical transformations at high temperatures. After that, the product will gradually be heated with controlled cooling using natural gas. This process stabilizes the brick structure.
6. Storage: The final product is packed for storage and ready for transportation and distribution.

C. Implemented Model for Local Context

The Business Process Model and Notation (BPMN) 2.0 is a standard graphical representation for business process modeling. Figure 2 is a diagram presenting the resource management process in SNG in three major steps after extraction/procurement and before sales/marketing, namely: Parc, Main Manufacturing (Production, Spare Parts Warehouse), and Storage. Parc is in charge of providing clay and sand to prepare the raw material, resolving shortages, and keeping track of such data. Main Manufacturing produces products and maintains quality by means of repair and inspection using the equipment provided by the Spare Parts Warehouse. After the control quality step, the qualified products are then forwarded to Storage. This will also enable IM levels in storage for sales later. Decision gateways, information flows, and data logging ensure synchronized communication and efficient workflow.

The reason why Smart Contracts are excellent for designing decentralized applications (DApps) to manage SNG resources is their security and automation of the execution of the agreement as a computer program. The immutability of the Blockchain ledger increases the confidence of every transaction of the recorded resources, hence it is tamper-proof and dispute-free. Blockchain with Smart Contracts revolutionize resource management by forcing accountability, cost reduction, and scalability.

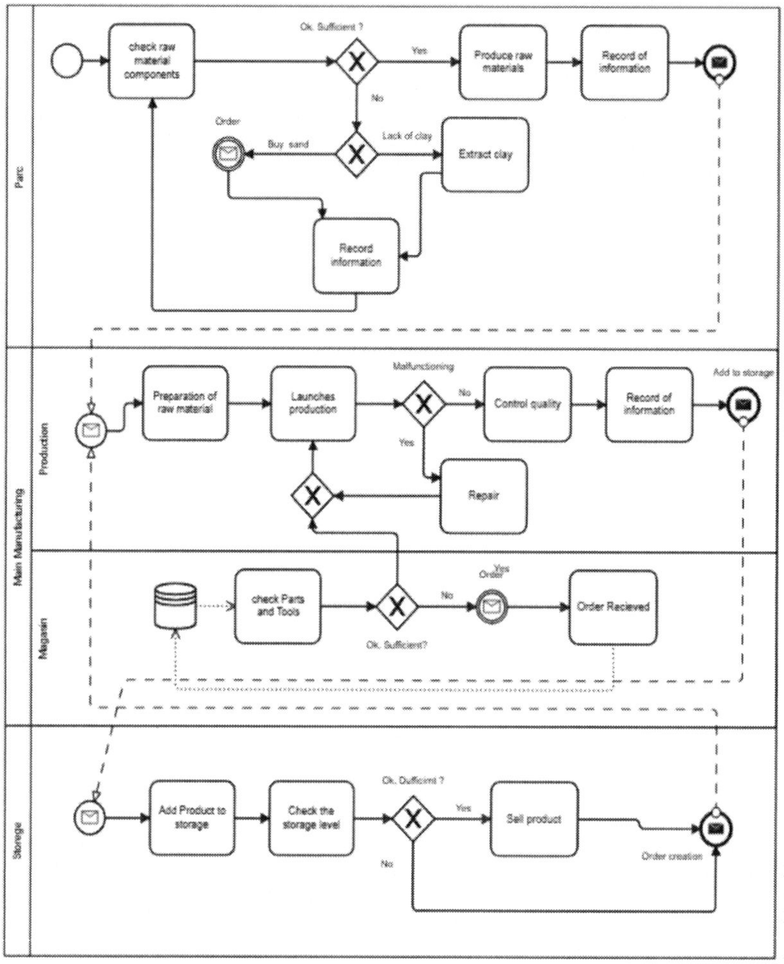

Figure 2. SNG's BPMN 2.0 Resource Management Diagram.

In this paper, we propose a model based on the combination of Smart Contracts based Blockchain with the goal of enhancing resources management in SNG while accounting for the shortcomings of SNG's traditional access data system. First, given the traditional nature of the factory, we propose several suggestions that help our DApps platform ensure effective and accurate management of resources and access data. One suggestion is to install smart sensors of different types (from truck weighbridge, to shape sensor, temperature and humidity sensors, etc.) that will display IoT data in real time at each stage of the process. Also, since the financial aspect of BC technology is prohibited in Algeria, we aim to overcome these constraints by theorizing solutions tailored to the factory's specific context. The decentralized application (DApp) is designed using a blockchain-based architecture (Figure 3), such as Ethereum. It employs smart contracts written in Solidity to automate various process functions [29], serving as the backend. Tools and libraries from the Node.js ecosystem, such as npm and Web3.js, are used to integrate the smart contracts into SNG's system.

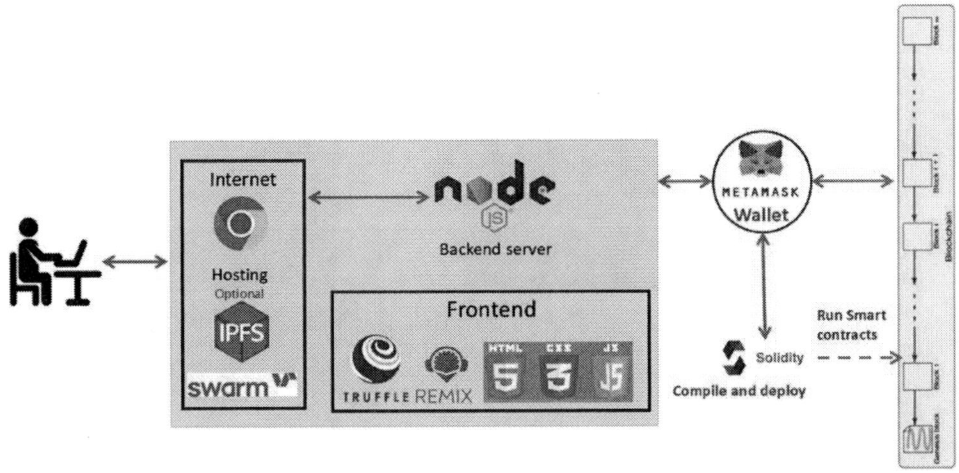

Figure 3. Architecture of our Decentralized Applications (DApps).

The decentralized application (DApp) primarily operates on-chain, ensuring transparency and immutability of core processes through smart contracts. To enhance scalability, efficiency, and reduce costs, we adopt a hybrid architecture that combines both on-chain and off-chain components (Figure 4). For secure decentralized storage, stakeholders can use communication protocols such as IPFS or Swarm. Users interact with the smart contracts through development environments like Remix IDE or Truffle. Additionally, we have developed a user-friendly web interface using HTML and JavaScript. All interactions between the blockchain and users are securely facilitated by a wallet application, such as MetaMask, which serves as a trusted intermediary.

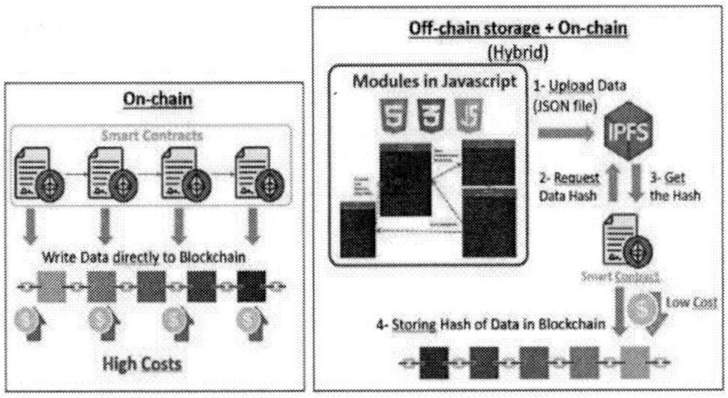

Figure 4. Architectures (On-Chain VS Hybrid).

D. *Implementation*

We used the Remix IDE, an online integrated development environment, to write, debug, and deploy smart contracts for resource management at SNG using Solidity on the Ethereum blockchain. Remix offers an intuitive interface with built-in tools for compilation, testing, and deployment, simplifying smart contract development [30].

As illustrated in Figure 5, the system comprises four main modules or interfaces: Magasin, Production, Parc, and Storage. The first three, Magasin, Parc, and Storage, share similar core functionalities, such as adding or removing items, updating quantities, and emitting events. However, they differ in terms of constructors, input parameters, and capacity constraints. Each module can also invoke specific functions, for example, the 'panne' function is triggered to indicate a malfunction.

The Magasin manages the inventory of tools, equipment, and spare parts used in the workshop. The Parc module handles the supply and tracking of raw materials such as sand and clay. Finally, the Storage module is responsible for the storage and sale of finished products, including "Brick 8" and "Brick 12". Finally, the Production module is dedicated to managing the manufacturing process of products such as Brick 8 and Brick 12. It utilizes external interfaces, namely IParc, IStock, and IMagasin, to interact with the other modules. Through these interfaces, it coordinates the consumption of raw materials, oversees the creation of finished goods, and updates inventory records accordingly.

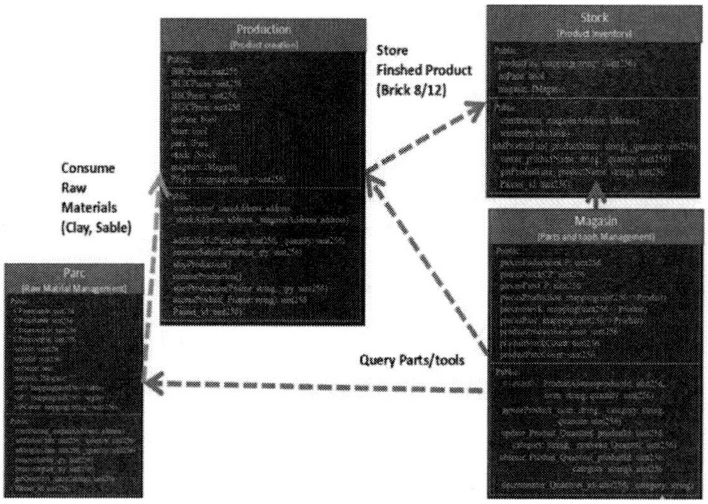

Figure 5. Simplified UML SNG resource management.

IV. Discussion and Challenges

Brick production often faces challenges related to traceability, cost control, and security. These issues underscore the potential advantages of adopting blockchain-based smart contract technology. In response, we developed a decentralized application (DApp) to manage the inventory system of the SNG brick factory, aiming to improve transparency, automation, and reliability in resource management.

Table III presents a concise comparison, based on our overall assessment, between PME Pro, the traditional application used at SNG, and the smart contract-based decentralized application at the resource management level. Traditional brick manufacturing processes typically rely on manual and centralized systems, which are time-consuming and susceptible to delays caused by intermediaries and outdated data. In contrast, our smart contract solution streamlines operations by automating workflows, supporting real-time decision-making, and minimizing the need for intermediaries. While traditional factories may consume less energy locally, blockchain networks require significantly more global energy due to their infrastructure requirements, including nodes and mining operations. However, it is important to note that several modern blockchain technologies, such as Avalanche and the upgraded Ethereum network, have significantly improved energy efficiency compared to earlier blockchain implementations. Smart contracts further enhance data security through decentralization and encryption, while also minimizing waste and fraud via precise tracking of assets and resources. Additionally, they facilitate seamless integration of communication protocols across departments and ensure transactional integrity. By eliminating intermediaries and reducing the risk of fraud or tampering, smart contracts offer a more secure and trustworthy alternative to traditional resource management methods.

TABLE III. COMPARISON PME PRO VS DAPPS

Resources Aspect	*PME Pro (Traditional Application's Brick Factory)*	*DApps with Smart Contracts (Solidity)*
Time consumption	High (Manual and delayed processes)	Low (Automated, real-time processes)
Cost	High (Intermediary costs)	Lower (Fewer intermediaries)
energy consumption	Low (Single factory operations)	High (ex: BC that uses Proof of Work, Public BC) Low (ex: BC that uses Proof of Stake, Privat BC, etc.)
Data	Centralized (Vulnerable)	Decentralized (Secure)
Physical waste	High (Ineffective tracking)	Low (Accurate tracking)
Communication	Fragmented communication across departments	Integrated and decentralized communications protocol
Automation	Manual	Automated
Risk Management	High	Low

Transaction history in our local blockchain, as an example of a smart contract, is crucial for optimizing resource management at brick factories by providing a transparent and immutable record of activities. It enables precise tracking of raw material purchases, energy consumption, and production outputs, leading to better resource allocation. Historical data also helps identify patterns, which can facilitate process improvements and reduce disputes. Additionally, transaction history supports compliance with regulations by maintaining a verifiable audit trail. It further allows the factory to forecast demand, plan inventory effectively, and avoid overstocking or shortages.

V. Conclusion and Future Works

This study highlights the transformative potential of BlockChain (BC) technology and smart contracts in addressing inefficiencies in industrial resource management, particularly within the brick manufacturing industry. Smart contracts add significant value to inventory management (IM) operations by automating processes and ensuring transparency and traceability in transactions. Consistent with previous research, we confirm that integrating both technologies can reduce costs and reliance on intermediaries, enhance operational efficiency, automate workflows, and ensure compliance with quality and safety regulations. The potential of smart contracts to optimize resource management across industries such as manufacturing is increasingly compelling. Furthermore, the use of decentralized applications (DApps) can foster improved collaboration among stakeholders while streamlining inventory and production management processes. To further enhance our work, several future directions can be considered:

- Integrating IoT sensors and real-time data logging to improve operational accuracy and synchronization.
- Exploring the use of green blockchain technologies to promote more sustainable industrial practices and foster environmentally conscious decision-making [31].
- Implementing and evaluating the system in other manufacturing sectors to assess scalability and adaptability.
- Incorporating Key Performance Indicators (KPIs) to support data-driven optimization of resource management.
- Comparing the proposed solution across different blockchain platforms, including Hyperledger and Solana, to evaluate performance, scalability, and suitability.

References

[1] M. Singh, R. Goyat, and R. Panwar, “Fundamental pillars for industry 4.0 development: implementation framework and challenges in manufacturing environment,” The TQM Journal, vol. 36, no. 1, pp. 288-309, 2024.

[2] C. F. Chien, P. C. Kuo, P. C. Sun, and H. A. Kuo, “Green production planning for circular supply chain and resource management: An empirical study for high-tech textile dyeing” Resources, Conservation and Recycling, vol. 204, pp. 107499, 2024.

[3] J. A. Floyd, I. D'Adamo, S. F. Wamba, and M. Gastaldi, “Competitiveness and sustainability in the paper industry: The valorisation of human resources as an enabling factor,” Computers & Industrial Engineering, vol. 190, pp. 110035, 2024.

[4] A. C. Prabhakar, “Driving economic prosperity: fostering job-oriented sustainable and inclusive development in India,” Open Journal of Business and Management, vol. 12, no. 4, pp. 2854-2885, 2024.

[5] S. Nakamoto, “Bitcoin: a peer-to-peer electronic cash system,” Satoshi Nakamoto, 2008.

[6] A. K. Tyagi, “Engineering applications of blockchain in this smart era,” in Enhancing Medical Imaging with Emerging Technologies, IGI Global, pp. 180-196, 2024.

[7] V. R. Boppana, “Industry 4.0: revolutionizing the future of manufacturing and automation,” Innovative Computer Sciences Journal, vol. 10, no. 1, 2024.

[8] P. Verma, R. Srivastava, and S. Kumar, “Blockchain technology: applications and challenges,” Blockchain for IoT Systems, pp. 1-12, 2025.

[9] F. Bassan and M. Rabitti, “From smart legal contracts to contracts on blockchain: an empirical investigation,” Computer Law & Security Review, vol. 55, pp. 106035, 2024.

[10] V. Veeramachaneni, “Decentralized trust management in Web 3.0: a comprehensive approach to network security,” Recent Innovations in Wireless Network Security, vol. 7, no. 1, pp. 9-26, 2025.

[11] F. Carreira, P. R. D. Cunha, J. Barata, and J. Estima, “Tamper-proof blockchain-based contracts for the carriage of goods by road,” in Proc. Int. Conf. on Information Systems Development (ISD), no. 32nd, pp. 1-6, Aug. 2024.

[12] M. I. Hossain, T. Steigner, M. I. Hussain, and A. Akther, “Enhancing data integrity and traceability in industry cyber physical systems (ICPS) through blockchain technology: a comprehensive approach,” arXiv preprint, arXiv:2405.04837, 2024.

[13] R. Agrawal, S. Singhal, and A. Sharma, “Blockchain and fog computing model for secure data access control mechanisms for distributed data storage and authentication using hybrid encryption algorithm,” Cluster Computing, pp. 1-16, 2024.

[14] T. O. Sanyaolu, A. G. Adeleke, C. F. Azubuko, and O. S. Osundare, “Harnessing blockchain technology in banking to enhance financial inclusion, security, and transaction efficiency,” International Journal of Scholarly Research in Science and Technology, vol. 5, no. 1, pp. 35-53, Aug. 2024.

[15] M. Naik, A. P. Singh, and N. R. Pradhan, “Decentralizing ride-sharing: a blockchain-based application with smart contract automation and performance analysis,” Multimedia Tools and Applications, pp. 1-28, 2024.

[16] P. Antonino, J. Ferreira, A. Sampaio, A. W. Roscoe, and F. Arruda, “A refinement-based approach to safe smart contract deployment and evolution,” Software and Systems Modeling, pp. 1-37, 2024.

[17] G. Sowmya, R. Sridevi, and S. G. Shiramshetty, “Transforming finance: exploring the role of blockchain and smart contracts,”in Fintech Applications in Islamic Finance: AI, Machine Learning, and Blockchain Techniques, IGI Global, pp. 255-271, 2024.

[18] E. Daraghmi, S. Jayousi, Y. Daraghmi, R. Daraghmi, and H. Fouchal, “Smart contracts for managing the agricultural supply chain: a practical case study,” IEEE Access, 2024.

[19] D. Dhillon, Diksha, and D. Mehrotra, “Smart contract vulnerabilities: exploring the technical and economic aspects,” in Blockchain Transformations: Navigating the Decentralized Protocols Era, Springer Nature Switzerland, pp. 81-91, 2024.

[20] T. Korkusuz Polat and E. Baran, “A blockchain-based Quality 4.0 application for warehouse management system,” Applied Sciences, vol. 14, no. 23, pp. 10950, 2024.

[21] D. K. Vaka, “Integrating inventory management and distribution: a holistic supply chain strategy,” The International Journal of Managing Value and Supply Chains, vol. 15, no. 2, pp. 13-23, 2024.

[22] S. Kadam, R. Senta, R. K. Sah, A. Sawant, and S. Jain, “Blockchain revolution: a new horizon for supply chain management in hotel industry,” in Proc. 2024 Int. Conf. on Emerging Smart Computing and Informatics (ESCI), IEEE, pp. 1-8, Mar. 2024.

[23] S. Mittal, "Framework for optimized sales and inventory control: a comprehensive approach for intelligent order management application," International Journal of Computer Trends and Technology, vol. 72, no. 3, pp. 61-65, 2024.

[24] H. Saraswat, M. Manchanda, and S. Jasola, "An efficient secure predictive demand forecasting system using Ethereum virtual machine," IET Blockchain, 2024.

[25] M. H. Rahman, B. C. Menezes, and R. Baldacci, "Exploring the role of blockchain technology, warehouse automation, smart routing, and cloud computing in logistics performance," Production & Manufacturing Research, vol. 12, no. 1, pp. 2393614, 2024.

[26] E. Groenewald and O. K. Kilag, "E-commerce inventory auditing: best practices, challenges, and the role of technology," International Multidisciplinary Journal of Research for Innovation, Sustainability, and Excellence (IMJRISE), vol. 1, no. 2, pp. 36-42, 2024.

[27] K. Bajar, A. Kamat, S. Shanker, and A. Barve, "Blockchain technology: a catalyst for reverse logistics of the automobile industry," Smart and Sustainable Built Environment, vol. 13, no. 1, pp. 133-178, 2024.

[28] L. Hong and D. N. Hales, "How blockchain manages supply chain risks: evidence from Indian manufacturing companies," The International Journal of Logistics Management, vol. 35, no. 5, pp. 1604-1627, 2024.

[29] V. Buterin, "A next-generation smart contract and decentralized application platform," White Paper, vol. 3, no. 37, pp. 2-1, 2014.

[30] "Remix Plugin Directory Documentation," Dec. 2020. [Online]. Available: https://remix-plugins-directory.readthedocs.io/_/downloads/en/latest/pdf/. [Accessed: Jan. 15, 2025].

[31] E. H. Grabsi, S. Aitouche, A. Boughrira, H. Aouag, H. Zermane, and K. Zireg, "Green blockchain and smart homes: a systematic review," in Proc. 2023 Int. Conf. on Decision Aid Sciences and Applications (DASA), IEEE, pp. 326-330, 2023.

VAULT: Verified Access Control for LLM-Based Knowledge Graph Querying

Maximilian Stäbler
Institute for AI Safety & Security
German Aerospace Center (DLR)
Ulm, Germany
maximilian.staebler@dlr.de

Tobias Müller
Industry-University Collaboration
SAP SE
Walldorf, Germany
tobias.mueller15@sap.com

Frank Köster
Institute for AI Safety & Security
German Aerospace Center (DLR)
Ulm, Germany
frank.koester@dlr.de

Chris Langdon
Drucker School of Business
Claremont Graduate University
Claremont (CA), USA
chris.langdon@cgu.edu

Abstract—**The exponential growth of unstructured textual data in enterprise environments has made automated knowledge graph generation essential for efficient information management. Although recent advances in natural language processing have enabled automated knowledge extraction, organizations face two critical challenges: maintaining domain specificity in knowledge representation and ensuring secure, role-based access to sensitive information. VAULT (Verified Access Control for Large Language Model (LLM)-Based Knowledge Graph Querying) presents a novel framework that combines ontology-driven knowledge extraction with dynamic access control mechanisms. The framework introduces three key innovations: (1) a configurable domain-driven node structure that enforces domain-specific knowledge organization through semantic validation, (2) a multitiered access control mechanism that implements both document-level restrictions and node-level visibility patterns, and (3) an LLM-powered inference engine that dynamically filters knowledge graph traversal based on user authorization levels. We implement our approach using a prototype system that demonstrates the automated conversion of natural language text into structured knowledge graphs while maintaining security constraints. Our experimental evaluation encompasses comprehensive testing across 16 different open-source LLMs, analyzing their performance under varying access control conditions and authorization levels. The results demonstrate the framework's effectiveness in maintaining information security while preserving query response quality across different access tiers. The adaptability of the framework makes it particularly valuable for industries handling sensitive information, such as healthcare, finance, and intellectual property management, where both domain specificity and information security are paramount. This paper contributes to the field by bridging the gap between generic knowledge graph generation and domain-specific requirements while providing empirical evidence for the effectiveness of multilevel access control in LLM-based knowledge systems.**

Keywords-Knowledge Graphs; Verified Roled-Based Access; LLM; Semantic Interoperability.

I. Introduction

The exponential growth of unstructured textual data in modern enterprises has created unprecedented challenges in the management of information and the extraction of knowledge [1][2][3]. Organizations face the complex task of transforming large amounts of unstructured documents into actionable structured knowledge while maintaining strict security protocols and access controls [4][5]. This challenge is particularly acute as enterprises increasingly rely on automated systems to process and analyze their data repositories [1] or automate their business processes [6]. In modern enterprises, Enterprise Resource Planning (ERP) systems usually provide an integrated and continuously updated view of the core business processes, while Enterprise Knowledge Management (EKM) systems refer to the systematic handling of an organization's information assets, ensuring that employees can efficiently access, share, and utilize knowledge. With the rise of Natural Language Processing (NLP), companies are integrating AI-driven tools into their ERP and EKM systems to improve knowledge retrieval, automate document processing, support decision-making, and process automation [6][7][8][9]. However, maintaining domain and business process specificity, as well as implementing secure, role-based access, are critical challenges, which we explore in more detail in the following.

A. Maintaining Domain Specificity

Comprising domain-specific information is especially challenging for general-purpose NLP models that are trained on broad, openly available datasets, which may not adequately capture the nuances, such as distinct terms or abbreviations of specialized domains [10]. Without proper customization to local domain-specific data and business process knowledge, these models risk generating inaccurate, misleading, or overly generic knowledge representations that do not align with domain-specific terminology, ontologies, or reasoning frameworks [11]. Given an enterprise context, context awareness of NLP-based systems is especially relevant to ensure accurate interpretation of ERP-specific business processes, data, and terminology, as generic models may introduce inaccuracies that could disrupt operations, decision-making, or even lead to harmful consequences for the business.

Recent works explored various ways to ensure domain specificity, such as fine-tuning local data, prompt engineering, and few-shot learning, Knowledge Graph (KG) integration, or building Retrieval-Augmented-Generation (RAG) pipelines

[12]. Each technique has its own specific challenges. Although fine-tuning requires substantial computing resources and can be costly [13], simple prompt engineering with few-shot learning may not generalize well and requires careful prompt design and testing, which need to be revisited when new documents are introduced to the data repositories [14]. Curating KGs requires domain experts and may be complex to maintain and update dynamically [15]. RAG retrieves unstructured text that may contain conflicting or imprecise domain knowledge and lacks the reasoning ability to connect concepts.

The choice of the customization approach depends on the underlying use case, needs, and domain [12]. In our work, we are focusing on *EKM*, in which employees require accurate domain-specific responses from corporate knowledge bases. Hence, it is crucial to reduce misinformation and systems need to accommodate fast-changing and growing data repositories. In the context of EKM, we leverage a combination of structured KGs and RAG with the rationale of combining the precision of structured KG-based retrieval with the low-cost, real-time adaptability of RAG pipelines. To ensure appropriate knowledge representation across various domains, we present a novel configurable ontology-driven node structure.

B. Secure, Role-Based Access Control

While recent advances in Large Language Models (LLMs) have revolutionized knowledge extraction capabilities, they have simultaneously introduced critical security concerns regarding information access and distribution [2][16]. Traditional RAG systems, while efficient at knowledge extraction, rarely address the crucial aspects of user permissions and access restrictions, creating significant security risks and compliance challenges [1][4]. This limitation becomes particularly problematic in the context of EKM. Given the example in which a company uses an internal NLP-based search engine for corporate documents, it is essential to prevent unauthorized access and unintentional return of restricted sensitive information. Restricting information access policies should be dynamically changeable based on varying roles, since, for example, an executive should have access to strategic reports for their responsible domain, while employees usually have a more restricted view due to compliance or other company policies. For example, if an employee prompts the internal NLP-based system to *"Show the latest NDA template"*, the system should retrieve only the *template* without showing any information regarding any related confidential legal disputes. Hence, to ensure each employee's access to knowledge relevant to their role without unnecessary noise, the underlying NLP systems should integrate predefined enterprise identity and access management policies to enforce appropriate access control. To solve this challenge, our aim is to use explicit KG rules to store the relationships between users, roles, and access permissions. More specifically, we propose a novel multitiered access control mechanism with document-level restrictions and node-level visibility patterns that allows dynamic filtering of KG traversals based on user authorization levels.

C. Research Contribution

Existing solutions can be categorized into two distinct types: those that focus on the extraction of generic knowledge without considering security implications, and those that implement rigid access control mechanisms that lack the flexibility required for domain-specific knowledge management. The absence of a unified framework that combines robust security measures with sophisticated knowledge extraction capabilities represents a significant gap in current EKM systems. To address these challenges, we present VAULT (Verified Access Control for LLM-Based KG Querying), a novel framework that integrates three key innovations.

- A configurable domain-driven node structure that enforces domain-specific knowledge organization through semantic validation, ensuring consistent and contextually appropriate knowledge representation across various enterprise domains.
- A sophisticated multi-tiered access control mechanism that implements both document-level restrictions and node-level visibility patterns, providing granular control over information access while maintaining system flexibility.
- An innovative inference engine powered by open-source LLMs that dynamically filters KG traversal based on user authorization levels, demonstrating the framework's effectiveness across eleven different open-source language models.

This research addresses the critical gap between automated knowledge extraction and security requirements by providing a comprehensive solution that maintains both domain specificity and information security. The framework particularly addresses the challenges of managing permissions across multiple integrated data sources while ensuring zero margin of error in access control implementation. Empirical validation across multiple open-source LLMs demonstrates the framework's robustness and adaptability, establishing a foundation for secure, domain-aware knowledge management systems in enterprise environments.

The remainder of the paper is structured as follows. In Section II, we present the related work, reviewing approaches in knowledge graph generation, role-based access control, integration of large language models in knowledge management, ontology-driven knowledge extraction, and existing limitations. Section III describes the system architecture and implementation of the VAULT framework, covering the knowledge extraction layer, the access control layer, and the query processing layer. Section IV provides the results of our experimental evaluation, detailing the setup and methodologies used, including human expert evaluation and automated metrics. Finally, we conclude our work and discuss future research directions in Section V.

II. Related Work

Recent advances in knowledge management systems have highlighted the importance of integrating structured knowledge with flexible access control mechanisms. This section examines key approaches across several critical areas relevant to secure KG generation and management.

A. KG Generation from Unstructured Text

The transformation of unstructured textual data into KGs has become increasingly vital for enterprise information management [2][3][17]. Current approaches typically employ a three-stage process: entity extraction, relationship identification, and graph construction. While traditional methods like OpenNRE [18] achieve only 61.4% accuracy, modern techniques like REBEL [19] have demonstrated success rates of up to 87%. A significant challenge remains in verifying whether the extracted information actually exists in the source documents, leading to the development of hybrid approaches that combine traditional extraction methods with LLM capabilities.

B. Role-based Access Control in KGs

Role-Based Access Control (RBAC) has emerged as a critical component in KG systems, particularly in enterprise environments [4]. Modern implementations simplify security management by grouping users into roles based on their tasks rather than assigning individual permissions. Recent research has expanded this concept to include multilevel access control mechanisms that implement document-level restrictions and node-level visibility patterns [20][21]. A notable advancement is the development of graph-based access control patterns that enable both open and closed security policies.

C. LLM Integration in Knowledge Management Systems

The integration of LLMs into knowledge management systems represents a transformative development in organizational knowledge management [22][23]. Current approaches focus on automating content creation, improving knowledge retrieval, and improving system efficiency. However, implementation presents significant challenges, particularly regarding customization requirements and system integration. Although LLM integration has shown potential to improve knowledge discovery and automated summarization capabilities, concerns persist about the reliability and accountability of LLM-generated content.

D. Ontology-driven Knowledge Extraction

Ontology-driven knowledge extraction has been identified as a crucial method to maintain domain specificity in knowledge representation [24]. Current systems employ ontologies as formal knowledge sources that can unambiguously represent task specifications and domain knowledge. This approach has been particularly effective in specialized domains where maintaining semantic accuracy is paramount.

E. Limitations in Existing Solutions

Several key limitations persist in current approaches:

1) Verification Challenges: Existing systems face difficulties in verifying the accuracy of LLM-extracted information, particularly in maintaining the clear provenance of extracted knowledge [25].
2) Access Control Granularity: Although RBAC systems provide fundamental security mechanisms, they often lack the flexibility required for complex organizational hierarchies and dynamic access requirements [4].
3) Integration Complexity: The integration of LLMs with existing knowledge management systems often requires extensive customization, which can disrupt established workflows [22].

Domain adaptation is another key challenge. Current ontology-driven approaches often require significant manual effort to adapt to new domains, limiting their scalability across different business contexts. These limitations underscore the need for a more integrated approach that combines the strengths of LLM-based extraction, robust access control mechanisms, and domain-specific ontological validation.

III. System Architecture and Implementation

VAULT employs a three-layer architecture designed to ensure secure and efficient knowledge extraction and management. Each layer serves a specific purpose in the pipeline, from raw text processing to secure knowledge delivery. An overview of the architecture is shown in Figure 1.

A. Knowledge Extraction Layer

The knowledge extraction layer implements a sophisticated pipeline to transform unstructured text into structured KG. The resulting KG is shown in Figure 3. This process occurs in several distinct stages:

- *Document Processing:* Source documents are initially segmented into manageable text chunks, with an optimal chunk size of 600 tokens to maximize the extraction efficiency of the entities.
- *Entity and Relationship Extraction:* The system performs entity and relationship extraction using LLM-based processing (either ChatGPT or local Ollama models) through multiple "gleaning" rounds for comprehensive coverage. Users can define domain-specific entities for mapping, ensuring relevance to their application area. The extraction uses a multipart prompt to identify entities (with name, type, and description) and their relationships, which can be customized through few-shot examples for specialized domains. The summarisation of community detection results is facilitated by LLM-based abstractive summarisation, thereby enabling both hierarchical data exploration and focused querying.
- *Community Detection:* In contrast with related work that exploits the structured retrieval and traversal affordances of graph indexes, the focus here is on a previously unexplored quality of graphs in this context: their inherent modularity [26] and the ability of community detection algorithms to partition graphs into modular communities of closely-related nodes (e.g., Leiden [27]). LLM-generated summaries of these community descriptions provide comprehensive coverage of the underlying graph

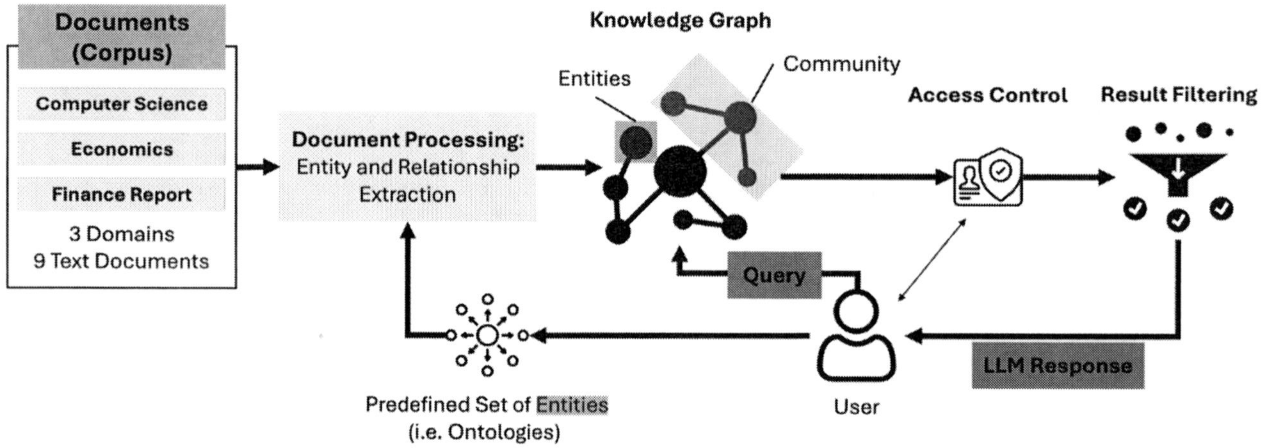

Figure 1. VAULT architecture overview: process from reading the input data, to building the KG, to generating a personalised access-controlled response to a user query. The user can specify a selection of entities to be used to build the KG.

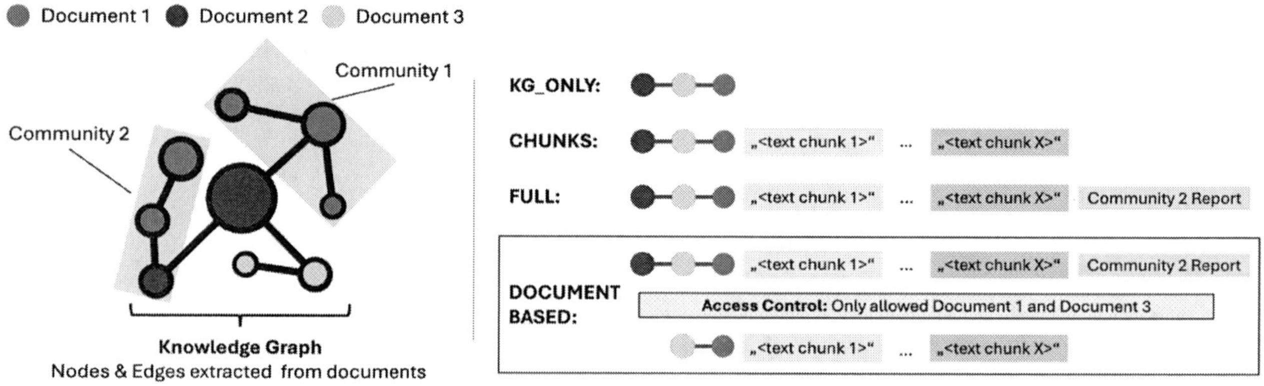

Figure 2. Overview of access levels: KG structure with predefined entities and Leiden-extracted communities. Responses are filtered based on user authorization, especially in the *DOCUMENT_BASED* mode.

index and the input documents it represents. Query-focused summarisation of an entire corpus is then facilitated through a map-reduce approach. This approach involves the use of each community summary to answer the query independently.

B. Access Control Layer

The Access Control Layer implements a sophisticated four-tier security system that provides granular control over knowledge access and retrieval. This hierarchical approach ensures precise information delivery while maintaining security boundaries across different user-authorization levels. An overview is given in Figure 2.

The system implements four distinct access levels:

1) *KG_ONLY*: Provides access exclusively to authorized nodes and edges within the KG that match the query parameters. This most restrictive level ensures visibility of the basic knowledge structure while maintaining strict information control.
2) *CHUNKS*: Extends the KG_ONLY access by including referenced text chunks from the original documents, enabling users to verify KG assertions through source material while maintaining security constraints.
3) *FULL*: Augments the CHUNKS level by incorporating community summaries derived from the KG structure. These summaries provide a contextual understanding of node clusters while preserving access control boundaries.
4) *DOCUMENT_BASED*: Implements a distinct approach where document access is determined by node-level permissions. The system first performs a FULL-level search, but then filters results based on user authorization for specific nodes associated with the extracted text.

This multitiered approach operates independently of the query processing layer, ensuring consistent security enforcement regardless of the underlying LLM implementation. The system validates access permissions before any content reaches the query processing stage, effectively creating a security boundary that prevents unauthorized information disclosure.

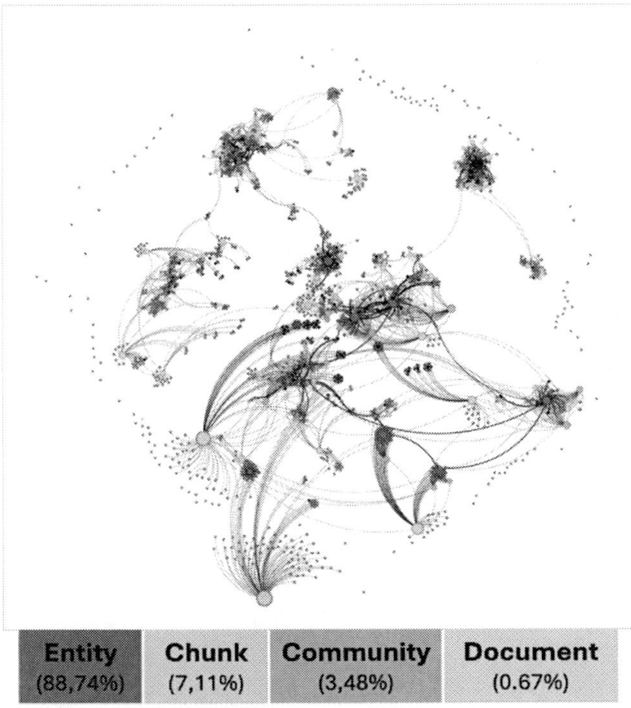

Figure 3. Visualisation of the KG extracted from the nine input documents and the predetermined entities.

The DOCUMENT_BASED level represents a particularly innovative approach, as it combines traditional document-level access control with node-based permissions, enabling fine-grained control over information flow while maintaining document context. This method ensures that users can access only the information from documents where they have appropriate authorization for the referenced KG nodes.

Each access level builds upon the previous one, creating a hierarchical security model that can accommodate various organizational security requirements while maintaining system flexibility. This layered approach enables organizations to implement precise access control policies while maximizing the utility of knowledge within authorized boundaries.

C. Query Processing Layer

The query processing layer utilizes a flexible LLM integration architecture that supports multiple open-source models through *Ollama*[28]. The implementation includes support for various models ranging from lightweight (1.5b parameters) to large-scale (32b parameters) architectures, including:

- *DeepSeek* models (1.5b and 32b variants)
- *Llama3.2* (1b and 3b)
- *Mistral-small* (24b)
- *Phi* variants (3.5b and 4b)
- *Qwen2.5* variants (0.5b to 7b)
- *SmolLM* series (135m to 1.7b)

The query processing implements a sophisticated retrieval and generation pipeline that leverages both the hierarchical community structure and the underlying KG. The system first identifies relevant entities through a semantic search, which serve as entry points for graph traversal. From these entry points, the system explores connected text chunks, community reports, and entity relationships, with all retrieved data being filtered according to the user's access level. The system employs a map-reduce approach to handle broad thematic queries. Retrieval of relevant community node reports from specified hierarchical levels, which are then shuffled and chunked. Each segment generates points with associated importance scores that are subsequently ranked and filtered to maintain the most significant information. This filtered intermediate response serves as a context for the final LLM-generated answer. This approach combines structured KG data with unstructured document content, enabling comprehensive responses that incorporate both specific entity information and broader thematic understanding. The community-based retrieval strategy has been shown to be particularly effective in addressing queries about broad themes and ideas, thus overcoming the limitations of traditional RAG methodologies in handling corpus-wide analysis.

The modular design of the system facilitates the seamless integration of new models while ensuring the consistent application of security controls across all configurations. Query processing is only initiated after access control validation, ensuring that responses are generated using only authorized information. This architecture enables VAULT to maintain strict security boundaries while leveraging the capabilities of modern LLMs for knowledge extraction and query processing. The implementation demonstrates both scalability and flexibility, accommodating various organizational security requirements while maintaining efficient knowledge management capabilities. The Knowledge Extraction Layer and the Query Processing Layer have been inspired by the Microsoft GraphRAG approach [29]. The complete implementation is available here [30].

IV. Results

This section presents the comprehensive evaluation of VAULT's performance across different access control configurations and LLM models.

A. Experimental Setup

We conducted an extensive evaluation using a diverse dataset comprising computer science papers and financial documents. The experiment included 20 carefully crafted questions derived from two distinct documents: a computer science research paper and Apple's SEC 8K report for 2024. The evaluation framework encompassed 16 open source language models deployed through Ollama, tested across four access control configurations with two different user roles, resulting in 2,240 unique question-response pairs.

B. Evaluation Methodology

The evaluation process consisted of two complementary approaches:

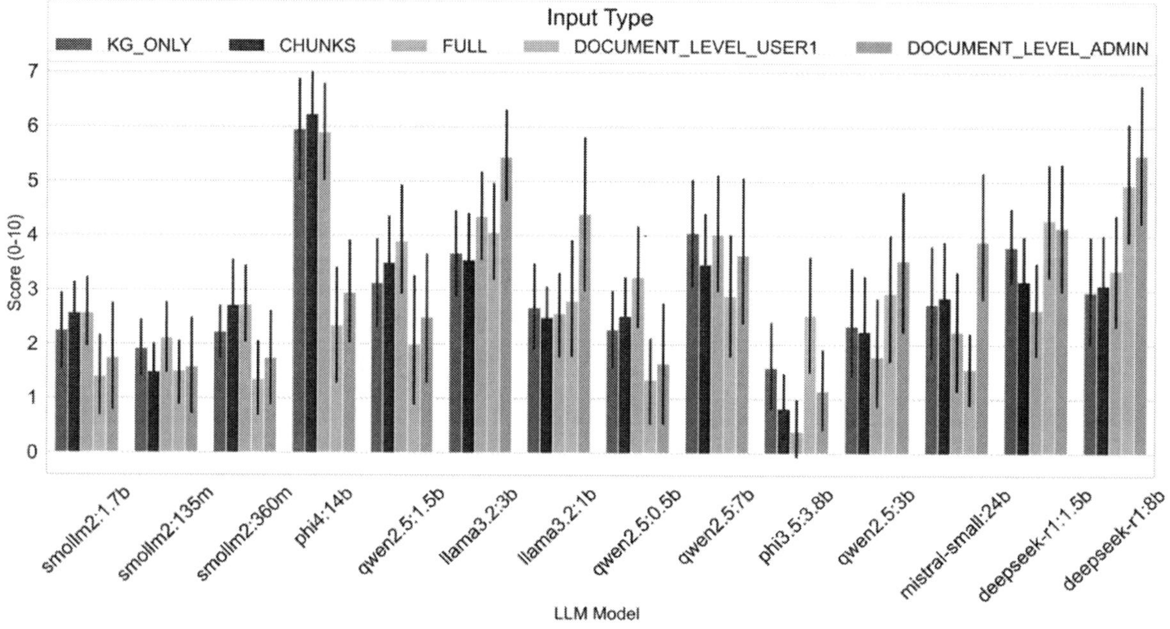

Figure 4. Visualization of the performance comparison across 16 different open-source LLM models with varying parameter sizes (135m to 8b) under different access control configurations. The y-axis represents the manual quality score (0-10), while the x-axis lists the different LLM models.

Human Expert Evaluation Eight researchers conducted systematic evaluations of responses, the evaluation corpus being equally divided between them. Each expert:

- Assigned a quality score (1-10 scale - higher is better)
- Provided qualitative justification for their scoring
- Verified response correctness within access control constraints

Automated Metric Analysis We used the *OPIK* framework by *CometML*[31] to calculate six key metrics:

- *LevenshteinRatio*: Quantifies response validity through string similarity comparison against reference text, identifying structural and content deviations
- *Answer Relevance*: Measures response alignment with query intent and appropriateness, independent of factual accuracy
- *Context Precision*: Evaluates the accuracy of context usage in responses, identifying information misalignment with the provided context
- *Context Recall*: Assesses completeness of context utilization, measuring inclusion of critical information from available context
- *Usefulness*: Scores practical value (0.0-1.0) based on completeness, clarity, and applicability of responses
- *Hallucination*: Identifies and quantifies information generation that is not supported by input context or access permissions.

Automated metrics provided objective measurements, while human evaluation offered nuanced qualitative insights into response effectiveness. The following sections present detailed analyses of the results in these evaluation dimensions, examining the effectiveness of different levels of access control and the performance variations among the LLM models tested. The experimental results in Figure 4 demonstrate varying performance across different LLM models and access control configurations. The *phi4* model emerges as the top performer, achieving scores between 6 and 7 across all access levels, significantly outperforming other models in the evaluation. This performance suggests that model size does not necessarily correlate directly with effectiveness in access-controlled knowledge retrieval tasks. Across the access control spectrum, *KG_ONLY*, *CHUNKS*, and *FULL* access levels exhibit relatively consistent performance patterns within each model, although with notable variations in absolute scores. The *DOCUMENT_LEVEL* access shows a clear differentiation between *USER1* and *ADMIN* permissions, with *ADMIN* consistently achieving higher scores. This pattern validates the effectiveness of the access control mechanisms implemented. The larger models, including *deepseek-rp (1.8b)* and *mistral-small (24b)*, demonstrate more stable performance at different access levels compared to their smaller counterparts. However, smaller models like *smollm2* variants show more pronounced variations in performance in different access configurations. The error bars indicate considerable variance in performance, particularly in models with larger parameter counts, suggesting that the size of the model may influence response consistency. The results also reveal that the *DOCUMENT_LEVEL_ADMIN* configuration generally achieves higher scores compared to *USER1* access, particularly evident in models like *llama3.2*

TABLE I. PERFORMANCE METRICS BY ACCESS TYPE

Access Type	RT	Score	Hall.	Rel.	Use.	Prec.	Rec.
DOCUMENT_LEVEL_ADMIN	**1.90**	**3.14**	**0.79**	**0.50**	0.47	**0.22**	**0.24**
FULL	3.24	3.00	0.91	0.46	0.48	0.17	0.18
KG_ONLY	3.18	2.97	0.90	0.48	**0.50**	0.19	0.20
CHUNKS	3.16	2.92	0.91	0.46	0.48	0.17	0.18
DOCUMENT_LEVEL_USER1	1.92	2.57	0.89	0.40	0.42	0.14	0.16

(3b) and *deepseek-r1*, indicating successful implementation of hierarchical access control mechanisms while maintaining response quality. A detailed analysis of performance metrics across access types, as shown in Table I, provides additional information on the effectiveness of the system. *DOCUMENT_LEVEL_ADMIN* configuration achieves the highest overall performance with a score of 3.14 and the lowest hallucination rate (0.79), indicating more reliable information retrieval. This configuration also demonstrates better precision (0.22) and recall (0.24) compared to other access levels, suggesting more accurate and comprehensive information extraction. Notably, while *KG_ONLY* access shows slightly lower overall scores (2.97), it achieves the highest usefulness metric (0.50), indicating that despite restricted access, responses remain practically valuable. *FULL* and *CHUNKS* access levels show similar performance patterns across the metrics, with scores of 3.00 and 2.92, respectively, suggesting that additional context beyond basic fragments may not significantly improve response quality. *DOCUMENT_LEVEL_USER1* consistently shows lower performance across all metrics, with the lowest overall score (2.57) and reduced relevance (0.40), confirming the effectiveness of access control mechanisms in restricting unauthorized information access. The response time (RT) metrics indicate that the $DOCUMENT\_LEVEL$ configurations (both *ADMIN* and *USER1*) process queries significantly faster (1.90 and 1.92 seconds, respectively) compared to other types of access, suggesting more efficient information retrieval when operating at the document level. These findings demonstrate that, while stricter access controls may limit overall information availability, they can lead to more precise and efficient information retrieval when properly implemented. The results also validate the system's ability to maintain security boundaries while preserving response quality within authorized access levels. Figure 5 presents a detailed analysis of the performance of the model in two key dimensions. The upper plot reveals a positive correlation between answer relevance and usefulness metrics, with most models clustering in the $0.4-0.7$ range for relevance and $0.3-0.6$ for usefulness. Notably, larger models like *qwen2.5:14b* and *mistral-small:24b* achieve higher scores on both metrics, while smaller models such as *deepseek-r1:1.5b* show lower performance. The lower plot examines the precision-recall relationship, where a distinct cluster of better performing models emerges in the upper right quadrant (precision: 0.25 – 0.30, recall: 0.22 – 0.32). This cluster, highlighted in the plot, predominantly consists of larger parameter models, suggesting that increased model size contributes to both higher precision and greater recall in knowledge retrieval tasks. Response times, indicated by dot sizes, remain relatively consistent across models, with no significant performance penalties for larger architectures. The visualization effectively demonstrates that while model size correlates with improved performance metrics, even smaller models can achieve competitive results, particularly in the midrange of the performance spectrum.

The effectiveness of VAULT's access control mechanisms is particularly evident when examining specific query responses - shown in Figure 6. Consider the question *"Who is Apple's new Chief Financial Officer?"* posed to the *mistral-small:24b* model under different access levels. When queried with *USER1* permissions, the model correctly responded with *"I don't have the information about who Apple's new Chief Financial Officer is,"* demonstrating appropriate handling of access restrictions, as the Apple SEC report was restricted to admin access only. In contrast, under *ADMIN* privileges, the same model provided a comprehensive response detailing Kevan Parekh's appointment as CFO, including contextual information about the transition and its implications for corporate governance. This stark contrast in response quality and content accuracy directly validates the effectiveness of access control implementation. Human evaluators noted this distinction, observing that *USER1* responses appropriately acknowledged information limitations, while *ADMIN* responses provided accurate and detailed information about Kevan Parekh's appointment. The *ADMIN* response not only identified the new CFO, but also provided valuable context about the leadership transition and its implications for Apple's financial management structure. This example effectively demonstrates VAULT's ability to:

- Maintain strict access control boundaries
- Prevent unauthorized information disclosure
- Provide comprehensive responses when appropriate access is granted
- Generate contextually appropriate responses based on access level

The significant difference in response quality and content between the *USER1* and *ADMIN* access levels validates the effectiveness of the framework in implementing secure, role-based access control while maintaining response quality within authorized boundaries.

V. Conclusion and Future Work

VAULT demonstrates effective integration of secure access control mechanisms with LLM-based knowledge graph generation and querying. The framework successfully addresses two critical challenges in enterprise knowledge management: maintaining domain specificity and implementing flexible access control. Through a comprehensive evaluation across

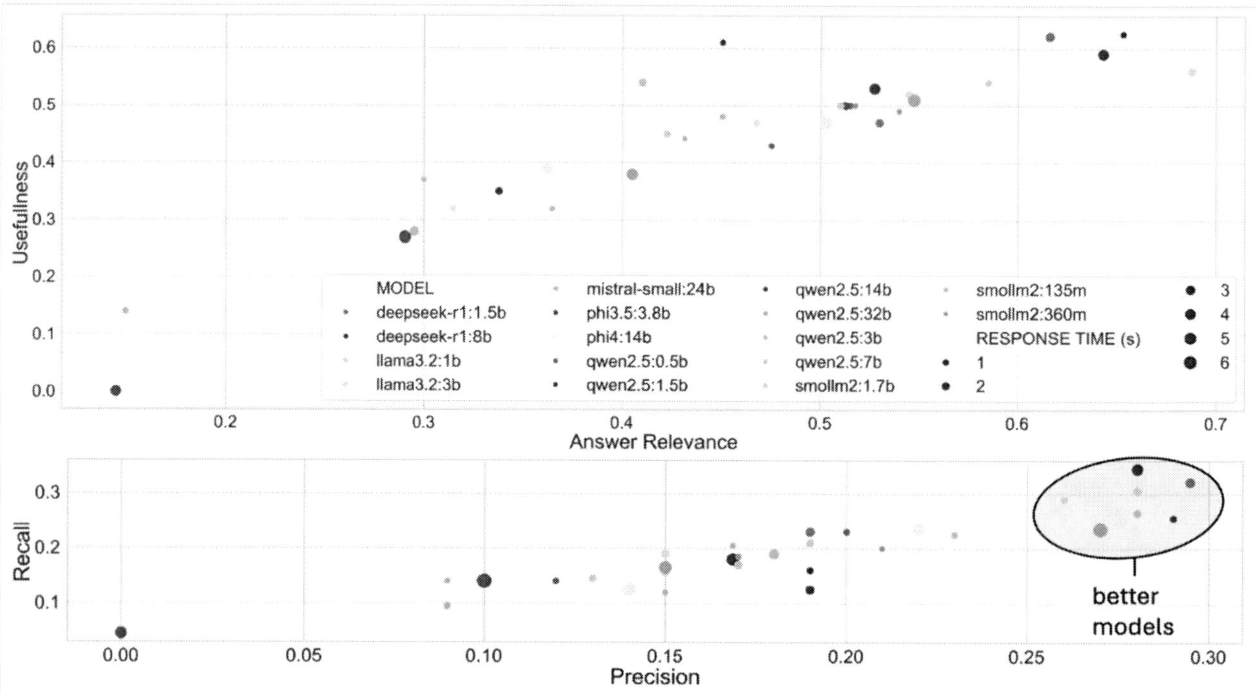

Figure 5. Open-Source-LLM Model comparison.

Figure 6. Comparison of VAULT responses across different access levels using the *mistral-small:24b model*. The figure shows the ground truth (left), admin-level response with admin access (center), and user1-level response with restricted access (right), demonstrating effective access control implementation.

16 different open-source LLMs and multiple access control configurations, we have demonstrated the system's ability to maintain information security while preserving query response quality. Key contributions of this work include the following.

- A configurable ontology-driven architecture that enables domain-specific knowledge organization
- A multi-tiered access control system that provides granular information access management
- An LLM-powered inference engine that effectively filters knowledge graph traversal based on authorization levels

The results show that the *DOCUMENT_LEVEL_ADMIN* setup performs best, with the highest score (3.14) and lowest hallucination rate (0.79), effectively balancing response quality and strict access control.

A. Future Work

Several promising directions for future research emerge from this work:

- *Dynamic Access Control*: Developing mechanisms for real-time adaptation of access control policies based on user behavior and organizational changes.
- *Cross-Domain Integration*: Extending the framework to handle multiple domain ontologies simultaneously, enabling more flexible knowledge integration across different business units.
- *Performance Optimization*: Investigating techniques to reduce response times

These future directions aim to enhance VAULT's practical applicability while maintaining its core strengths in secure, domain-specific knowledge management.

References

[1] W. Fan *et al.*, "A Survey on RAG Meeting LLMs: Towards Retrieval-Augmented Large Language Models," in *Proceedings of the 30th ACM SIGKDD Conference on Knowledge Discovery and Data Mining*, Barcelona Spain: ACM, Aug. 2024, pp. 6491–6501, ISBN: 9798400704901. DOI: 10.1145/3637528.3671470.

[2] B. Peng *et al.*, "Graph Retrieval-Augmented Generation: A Survey," Sep. 2024. DOI: 10.48550/arXiv.2408.08921. arXiv: 2408.08921 [cs].

[3] K. Pichai, "A Retrieval-Augmented Generation Based Large Language Model Benchmarked On a Novel Dataset," *Journal of Student Research*, vol. 12, no. 4, Nov. 2023, ISSN: 2167-1907. DOI: 10.47611/jsrhs.v12i4.6213.

[4] K. Jagannath, "Enhancing Retrieval-Augmented Generation with Permissions Awareness," *Defensive Publications Series*, May 2024.

[5] K. Sawarkar, A. Mangal, and S. R. Solanki, *Blended RAG: Improving RAG (Retriever-Augmented Generation) Accuracy with Semantic Search and Hybrid Query-Based Retrievers*, Aug. 2024. DOI: 10.48550/arXiv.2404.07220. arXiv: 2404.07220 [cs].

[6] J. Schnepf, T. Engin, S. Anderer, and B. Scheuermann, "Studies on the Use of Large Language Models for the Automation of Business Processes in Enterprise Resource Planning Systems," in *Natural Language Processing and Information Systems*, A. Rapp, L. Di Caro, F. Meziane, and V. Sugumaran, Eds., Cham: Springer Nature Switzerland, 2024, pp. 16–31, ISBN: 978-3-031-70239-6. DOI: 10.1007/978-3-031-70239-6_2.

[7] P. M. Mah, I. Skalna, and J. Muzam, "Natural Language Processing and Artificial Intelligence for Enterprise Management in the Era of Industry 4.0," *Applied Sciences*, vol. 12, no. 18, p. 9207, Jan. 2022, ISSN: 2076-3417. DOI: 10.3390/app12189207.

[8] M. V. Godbole, "Revolutionizing Enterprise Resource Planning (ERP) Systems through Artificial Intelligence," *International Numeric Journal of Machine Learning and Robots*, vol. 7, no. 7, pp. 1–15, Dec. 2023.

[9] P. Pokala, *The Integration And Impact Of Artificial Intelligence In Modern Enterprise Resource Planning Systems: A Comprehensive Review*, SSRN Scholarly Paper, Rochester, NY, Nov. 2024. DOI: 10.2139/ssrn.5069295. Social Science Research Network: 5069295.

[10] K. Pakhale, *Comprehensive Overview of Named Entity Recognition: Models, Domain-Specific Applications and Challenges*, Sep. 2023. DOI: 10.48550/arXiv.2309.14084. arXiv: 2309.14084 [cs].

[11] Y. Li *et al.*, *Personal LLM Agents: Insights and Survey about the Capability, Efficiency and Security*, May 2024. DOI: 10.48550/arXiv.2401.05459. arXiv: 2401.05459 [cs].

[12] C. Ling *et al.*, *Domain Specialization as the Key to Make Large Language Models Disruptive: A Comprehensive Survey*, Mar. 2024. DOI: 10.48550/arXiv.2305.18703. arXiv: 2305.18703 [cs].

[13] A. Balaguer *et al.*, *RAG vs Fine-tuning: Pipelines, Tradeoffs, and a Case Study on Agriculture*, Jan. 2024. DOI: 10.48550/arXiv.2401.08406. arXiv: 2401.08406 [cs].

[14] Z. Zhang *et al.*, *Personalization of Large Language Models: A Survey*, May 2025. DOI: 10.48550/arXiv.2411.00027. arXiv: 2411.00027 [cs].

[15] H. Abu-Rasheed, C. Weber, and M. Fathi, "Knowledge Graphs as Context Sources for LLM-Based Explanations of Learning Recommendations," in *2024 IEEE Global Engineering Education Conference (EDUCON)*, May 2024, pp. 1–5. DOI: 10.1109/EDUCON60312.2024.10578654. arXiv: 2403.03008 [cs].

[16] J. Liu, J. Lin, and Y. Liu, *How Much Can RAG Help the Reasoning of LLM?* Oct. 2024. DOI: 10.48550/arXiv.2410.02338. arXiv: 2410.02338 [cs].

[17] H. N. Patel, A. Surti, P. Goel, and B. Patel, "A Comparative Analysis of Large Language Models with Retrieval-Augmented Generation based Question Answering System," in *2024 8th International Conference on I-SMAC (IoT in Social, Mobile, Analytics and Cloud) (I-SMAC)*, Kirtipur, Nepal: IEEE, Oct. 2024, pp. 792–798, ISBN: 9798350376425. DOI: 10.1109/I-SMAC61858.2024.10714814.

[18] X. Han *et al.*, "OpenNRE: An Open and Extensible Toolkit for Neural Relation Extraction," in *Proceedings of the 2019 Conference on Empirical Methods in Natural Language Processing and the 9th International Joint Conference on Natural Language Processing (EMNLP-IJCNLP): System Demonstrations*, Hong Kong, China: Association for Computational Linguistics, 2019, pp. 169–174. DOI: 10.18653/v1/D19-3029.

[19] A. Gupte *et al.*, *REBEL: Rule-based and Experience-enhanced Learning with LLMs for Initial Task Allocation in Multi-Human Multi-Robot Teams*, Sep. 2024. DOI: 10.48550/arXiv.2409.16266. arXiv: 2409.16266 [cs].

[20] V. A. Batista, D. S. M. Gomes, and A. G. Evsukoff, *SESAME - Self-supervised framework for Extractive queStion Answering over docuMent collEctions*, Mar. 2024. DOI: 10.21203/rs.3.rs-4018202/v1.

[21] S. Setty, H. Thakkar, A. Lee, E. Chung, and N. Vidra, *Improving Retrieval for RAG based Question Answering Models on Financial Documents*, Aug. 2024. DOI: 10.48550/arXiv.2404.07221. arXiv: 2404.07221 [cs].

[22] X. Zhou, X. Zhao, and G. Li, *LLM-Enhanced Data Management*, Feb. 2024. DOI: 10.48550/arXiv.2402.02643. arXiv: 2402.02643 [cs].

[23] B. P. Allen, L. Stork, and P. Groth, *Knowledge Engineering using Large Language Models*, Oct. 2023. DOI: 10.48550/arXiv.2310.00637. arXiv: 2310.00637 [cs].

[24] D. Dua, E. Strubell, S. Singh, and P. Verga, "To Adapt or to Annotate: Challenges and Interventions for Domain Adaptation in Open-Domain Question Answering," in *Proceedings of the 61st Annual Meeting of the Association for Computational Linguistics (Volume 1: Long Papers)*, Toronto, Canada: Association for Computational Linguistics, 2023, pp. 14 429–14 446. DOI: 10.18653/v1/2023.acl-long.807.

[25] S. Siriwardhana *et al.*, "Improving the Domain Adaptation of Retrieval Augmented Generation (RAG) Models for Open Domain Question Answering," *Transactions of the Association for Computational Linguistics*, vol. 11, pp. 1–17, Jan. 2023, ISSN: 2307-387X. DOI: 10.1162/tacl_a_00530.

[26] M. E. J. Newman, *Modularity and community structure in networks*, https://www.pnas.org/doi/epdf/10.1073/pnas.0601602103, 2006. DOI: 10.1073/pnas.0601602103.

[27] V. Traag, L. Waltman, and N. J. van Eck, "From Louvain to Leiden: Guaranteeing well-connected communities," *Scientific Reports*, vol. 9, no. 1, p. 5233, Mar. 2019, ISSN: 2045-2322. DOI: 10.1038/s41598-019-41695-z. arXiv: 1810.08473 [cs].

[28] *Ollama*, https://ollama.com.

[29] D. Edge *et al.*, *From Local to Global: A Graph RAG Approach to Query-Focused Summarization*, Apr. 2024. DOI: 10.48550/arXiv.2404.16130. arXiv: 2404.16130 [cs].

[30] *Code Implementation*, https://tinyurl.com/43zb4duk.

[31] *Opik LLM development Platform | Observability, Evaluation & Security*, https://www.comet.com/docs/opik.

Stance-Conditioned Modeling for Rumor Verification

Gibson Nkhata, Susan Gauch
Department of Electrical Engineering and Computer Science
University of Arkansas
Fayetteville, AR 72701, USA
e-mails: {gnkhata, sgauch}@uark.edu

***Abstract*—The rapid spread of misinformation on social media platforms has heightened the need for effective rumor verification models. Traditional approaches primarily rely on textual content and transformer-based embeddings, but they often fail to incorporate conversational dynamics and stance evolution, limiting their effectiveness. We present a stance-conditioned rumor verification model that integrates Bidirectional Encoder Representations from Transformers (BERT) based source post embeddings, reply post embedding aggregation, and Bidirectional Long Short Term Memory (BiLSTM) encoding of stance labels to enhance rumor classification. By explicitly modeling stance progression and leveraging aggregated stance-conditioned reply embeddings, our approach captures critical discourse patterns that influence rumor veracity. Experiments on competitive benchmark tasks demonstrate that our model outperforms state-of-the-art baselines in Macro-F1 and accuracy, achieving superior performance across multiple datasets. Ablation studies confirm the effectiveness of each constituent model component, with early rumor detection analysis showcasing our model's ability to detect misinformation faster and more accurately than competing methods. Overall, this work presents a novel stance-conditioned approach to rumor verification that effectively captures conversational context and discourse interactions, providing a more robust and interpretable framework for combating online misinformation.**

Keywords-Rumor verification; stance-conditioned modeling; social media misinformation; embedding aggregation.

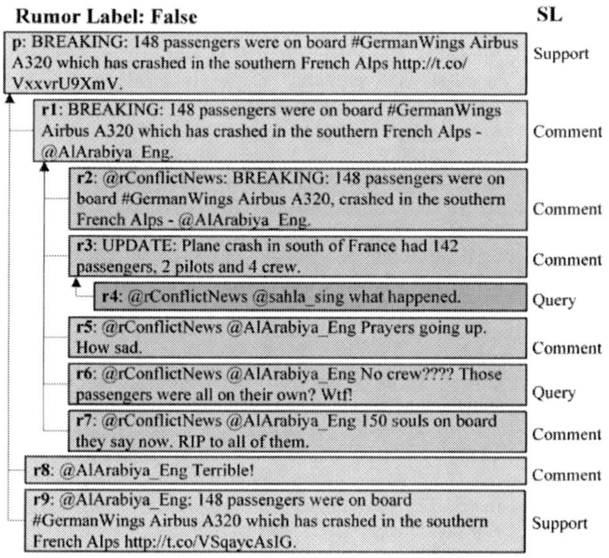

Figure 1. A sample thread C with a false veracity label. SL stands for Stance Labels.

I. Introduction

The exponential rise of social media platforms such as Twitter (rebranded as X) and Reddit has fueled the rapid spread of misinformation and rumors [1][2], making rumor verification a critical challenge. Traditional approaches primarily rely on transformer-based language models, such as Bidirectional Encoder Representations from Transformers (BERT) and Generative Pre-trained Transformer (GPT) [3][4] to analyze textual representations of posts. However, these methods often truncate conversational threads due to sequence length constraints and overlook valuable discourse signals, such as stance labels, that reflect user perspectives on rumors.

This work presents an enhanced rumor verification framework that effectively integrates the structure and stance dynamics of online discussions. Our approach builds upon prior work by incorporating stance labels as additional input features, embedded using a Bidirectional Long Short-Term Memory (BiLSTM) [5] network. Specifically, we extract source post embeddings using BERT [6] and concatenate them with stance-conditioned reply embeddings, where stance labels are sequentially modeled based on their temporal order in the conversation thread. The resulting feature representations are processed through a unified feed-forward layer for final classification.

Unlike prior studies that primarily rely on direct textual features [7][8], our model explicitly encodes stance signals, allowing it to capture the argumentative structure within rumor propagation. By preserving the full conversational context and avoiding truncation, our model offers a more holistic understanding of rumor veracity. Empirical results on benchmark rumor datasets demonstrate that our method significantly improves performance distinguishing rumor veracity classes, setting a new benchmark for rumor detection systems.

Furthermore, this study explores the task of early rumor detection, that focuses on identifying and assessing the veracity of emerging rumors in real-time as they propagate online. By detecting rumors at an early stage, this approach aims to mitigate the rapid spread of misinformation, enabling timely interventions and fact-checking before false narratives gain widespread traction. Figure 1 presents a sample discourse, showcasing how stances evolve. We leverage the evolution to model the temporal ordering of stance annotations with BiLSTM. The major contributions of this work are outlined as follows:

- **Novel rumor verification framework**: Presents a methodology that integrates BERT-based post embeddings and BiLSTM-based stance encoding to enhance rumor verification in conversational threads.
- **Avoiding sequence truncation**: Unlike prior approaches that truncate long conversation threads due to BERT's sequence length constraints, our model effectively aggregates embeddings without discarding crucial discourse information.
- **Leveraging stance labels**: Incorporates stance labels as an additional input feature, embedding them using a BiLSTM to capture the sequential stance evolution within a thread.
- **Early rumor detection**: Evaluates the model's ability to detect rumors at an early stage of the conversation, highlighting its real-world applicability for misinformation mitigation.

The rest of this paper unfolds as follows. Section II reviews the existing literature on rumor verification, and Section III delves into a comprehensive description of our approach. Section IV demonstrates experiments and provides a discussion of results. Finally, Section V presents the conclusion.

II. Related work

The proliferation of misinformation on social media has led to extensive research in rumor verification. Early studies primarily focused on content-based analysis, utilizing textual features and user metadata to assess veracity. Nonetheless, these approaches often overlooked the dynamic nature of conversations and the valuable insights provided by user stances within discussion threads.

Recently, Yang et al. [9] introduced a weakly supervised propagation model that leverages multiple instance learning for joint rumor verification and stance detection. This approach models the diffusion of claims through bottom-up and top-down trees, capturing the propagation structure of rumors. The model requires only bag-level labels concerning a claim's veracity, reducing the need for extensive labeled data. Experiments demonstrated promising performance in both claim-level rumor detection and post-level stance classification. Furthermore, Mai et al. [10] introduces a graph attention mechanism to effectively capture and process interactions within a conversational thread.

Jami et al. [11] conducted a comprehensive literature review on rumor stance classification in online social networks. They highlighted the importance of user viewpoints in predicting rumor veracity and discussed various approaches, datasets, and challenges in the field. The study emphasized the need for models that effectively utilize user stances to improve rumor verification systems.

Moreover, Khandelwal [12] explored a multi-task learning framework that jointly predicts rumor stance and veracity. By fine-tuning the Longformer model, the study addressed the limitations of sequence length in traditional transformer models, allowing for the processing of longer conversational threads without truncation. This approach underscored the benefits of handling extended contexts in rumor verification tasks.

Despite these advancements, challenges remain in effectively modeling the temporal dynamics of conversations and fully leveraging stance information. In addition, most of these models still suffer from sequence length limitations (since they rely on pretrained language models), often truncating crucial replies within a discourse. Our framework aims to address these gaps by proposing a sequential stance aggregation mechanism that accounts for the temporal ordering of replies and embedding stance labels using a BiLSTM [5] network, preserving the chronological order of replies. This method seeks to capture the evolution of discussions more effectively, providing a comprehensive understanding of rumor propagation and verification.

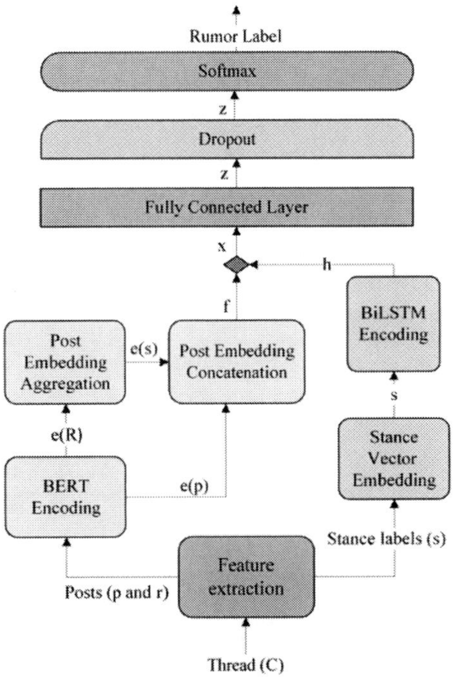

Figure 2. The model framework. $e(R)$, $e(p)$, and $e(s)$ represent e_R, e_p and e_s, respectively, in the main text.

III. Methodology

Our model consists of three main components: 1) **Post embedding representation**: BERT extracts contextual embeddings for the source and reply posts. 2) **Stance-aware sequence encoding**: A BiLSTM encodes the sequence of stance labels in temporal order. 3) **Unified feed-forward layer**: The post embeddings and stance representations are concatenated and fed into a classifier. Figure 2 illustrates our methodology.

A. Task Formulation

Given a conversational thread C (see Figure 1) consisting of a source post p and a set of reply posts $R = \{r_1, r_2, ..., r_n\}$, where n is the total number of reply posts, the goal of rumor verification is to classify the source post p into one of three categories: $y_c \in \{\text{true rumor}, \text{false rumor}, \text{unverified rumor}\}$. Each post (both p and r_i) is associated with a stance label s_i, where $s_i \in \{\text{support}, \text{deny}, \text{query}, \text{comment}\}$.

B. Post Embedding Representation and Aggregation

Each post x_i (both p and r_i) is tokenized and passed through a pre-trained BERT model. The mean-pooled hidden states are used as the post embedding:

$$\mathbf{e}_i = \text{BERT}(x_i) = \frac{1}{T}\sum_{t=1}^{T} h_t \tag{1}$$

where h_t represents the hidden state at position t of a given post, and T is the sequence length.

The source post embedding is:

$$\mathbf{e}_p = \text{BERT}(p) \tag{2}$$

The reply post embeddings are:

$$\mathbf{E}_R = \{\mathbf{e}_{r_1}, \mathbf{e}_{r_2}, ..., \mathbf{e}_{r_N}\} \tag{3}$$

To preserve stance information, we aggregate reply embeddings based on stance labels:

$$\mathbf{e}_s = \sum_{r_i \in R_s} \mathbf{e}_{r_i} \tag{4}$$

where R_s represents the set of replies with stance s. After aggregating embeddings for all four stances, these vectors are concatenated with the embedding of the source post to create a composite feature vector:

$$f = [e_p; e_s; e_d; e_q; e_c], \tag{5}$$

where subscripts (p, s, d, q, c) represent (source, support, deny, query, comment). Aggregating embeddings by stance allows the model to capture the distribution of opinions within a conversation thread. This method emphasizes the collective influence of each stance category, providing nuanced insights into the overall sentiment and credibility of the information. Prior research has highlighted the importance of analyzing specific stances, such as denial and questioning, in rumor detection, as they play a crucial role in assessing veracity [13]. On the same note, embedding aggregation addresses the challenge of thread sequence truncation, a common limitation in large language model-based approaches. By aggregating embeddings in this manner, the model can better discern patterns indicative of true, false, or unverified rumors.

C. Stance Label Encoding Using BiLSTM

Recent studies have demonstrated the efficacy of BiLSTMs in stance detection tasks. For instance, Jia et al. [14] proposed an improved BiLSTM approach that integrates external commonsense knowledge and environmental information to enhance user stance detection. Their method effectively captures the temporal progression of user viewpoints, leading to improved detection performance. Deviating from their approaches, in this work, each reply's stance label is first embedded into a continuous vector space:

$$\mathbf{s}_i = \text{Embed}(s_i) \tag{6}$$

These embedded stance vectors are then processed chronologically through a BiLSTM network:

$$\overrightarrow{h}_i, \overleftarrow{h}_i = \text{BiLSTM}(\mathbf{s}_i) \tag{7}$$

The final stance representation is obtained from the last hidden states:

$$\mathbf{h}_S = [\overrightarrow{h}_N; \overleftarrow{h}_N] \tag{8}$$

The utilization of a BiLSTM for encoding stance labels offers three primary advantages in this study. First, **capturing sequential dependencies**: conversations on social media often exhibit temporal dynamics, where the stance of a reply can influence and be influenced by preceding and subsequent replies. A BiLSTM processes the sequence in both forward and backward directions, effectively capturing these dependencies. This bidirectional processing ensures that the context from both past and future replies is considered, leading to a more comprehensive understanding of the stance dynamics within a thread. Next, **handling variable-length sequences**: social media threads vary in length and complexity. BiLSTMs are adept at managing such variability, allowing the model to process each thread appropriately without the need for strict length constraints. Finally, **enhanced contextual representation**: by encoding stance labels through a BiLSTM, the model generates contextually enriched representations that encapsulate the interplay between different stances over the course of the conversation. This enriched representation aids in distinguishing subtle nuances in stance expressions, that is crucial for accurate rumor verification.

D. Classification Layer

The final input to the classifier is the concatenation of the source post embedding, aggregated reply embeddings, and stance representation:

$$\mathbf{x} = [f; \mathbf{h}_S] \tag{9}$$

The classification module comprises a fully connected layer that projects the high-dimensional representation x onto the output space corresponding to the rumor classes (True, False, Unverified):

$$\mathbf{z} = \text{Dropout}\left(\mathbf{Wx} + \mathbf{b}\right), \tag{10}$$

where $\mathbf{W} \in \mathbb{R}^{C \times D}$ is a learnable weight matrix responsible for transforming the hidden representation $\mathbf{x}$ into the output space of C classes, and $\mathbf{b} \in \mathbb{R}^{C}$ denotes the bias term. Here, D represents the dimensionality of $\mathbf{x}$, while the number of classes is given by $C = 3$. *Dropout* is used for regularization. The raw output $\mathbf{z}$ is subsequently passed through a softmax activation function to derive class probabilities:

$$\hat{y}_i = \text{softmax}(\mathbf{z_i}) = \frac{\exp(z_i)}{\sum_{j=1}^{C}\exp(z_j)}, \quad i = 1, \ldots, C, \tag{11}$$

where $\hat{y}_i$ represents the predicted probability for class i.

E. Training and Optimization Objective

The training process involves computing the discrepancy between the predicted probabilities $\hat{y}$ and the true labels using the cross-entropy loss function:

$$\mathcal{L} = -\sum_{i=1}^{C} y_i \log(\hat{y}_i), \tag{12}$$

where y_i corresponds to the one-hot encoded ground truth label. The objective function for rumor verification aims to minimize the classification loss $\mathcal{L}$. The overall optimization seeks to enhance the model's ability to accurately classify rumor veracity. The objective function is expressed in detail as:

$$\mathcal{J}(\mathbf{y}, \hat{\mathbf{y}}) = -\frac{1}{N}\sum_{i=1}^{N}\sum_{c=1}^{C} y_{i,c} \log \hat{y}_{i,c}, \tag{13}$$

where N is the total number of rumor events in a training batch.

IV. Experiments

This section assesses the performance of our model in comparison to state-of-the-art (SOTA) baselines and conducts a comprehensive analysis to gain deeper insights into the model's effectiveness.

A. Datasets

Experiments are conducted on three widely used and publicly available challenging benchmark datasets: SemEval-2017 [15], RumorEval-2019 [2], and PHEME [16]. Among these, RumorEval-2019 and PHEME extend the SemEval-2017 task, that comprises 325 rumor-related events and 5,568 tweets collected from eight major breaking news events.

RumorEval-2019 extends SemEval-2017 by incorporating additional test data and new Reddit-based content while utilizing all SemEval-2017 rumor events for training. It consists of 446 rumor-related conversational threads and a total of 8,574 posts. The claims in both SemEval-2017 and RumorEval-2019 are annotated with three veracity labels: True, False, or Unverified. Each post within a thread is assigned a stance label: Support, Deny, Query, or Comment. Conversely, PHEME enhances RumorEval-2017 by incorporating additional rumor events and data from nine major breaking news stories on Twitter. It contains 2,402 conversational threads and 105,354 tweets. Unlike RumorEval-2019, the additional data in PHEME is annotated solely with rumor veracity labels.

For SemEval-2017 and RumorEval-2019, we adhere to the standard train/validation/test split as defined in the original publications. Conversely, since PHEME does not provide an official dataset split, a conventional evaluation protocol is adopted, that follows a leave-one-out k-fold validation strategy, where each event is used as a test set in turn. Table I provides a detailed summary of the dataset statistics.

B. Data Preprocessing

In addition to standard data preprocessing techniques, such as the removal of null entries, this work employs hashtag processing and text normalization following the methodology proposed by [17]. Furthermore, inspired by the approach of [18], all hyperlinks in the text are replaced with \$url\$ and all *@user* mentions are substituted with \$mention\$, as these transformations have been shown to enhance model performance in the aforementioned studies.

C. Experimental settings

The uncased-BERT-base version is employed to generate word embeddings for both the claim p and its corresponding replies R within a thread C. An alternative pre-trained language model, RoBERTa [19], was also evaluated; still, this model exhibited inferior performance compared to BERT and was thus excluded. Extensive experimentation with different hyperparameter settings was performed to identify the optimal configuration. The training process is conducted with a batch size of 16 threads, and the BERT tokenizer is configured with a maximum sequence length of 128. Optimization is carried out using the Adam optimizer [20] with a learning rate of 0.001. Dropout rate was set to 0.35. BiLSTM embedding dimension is set to (18, 19, 20) for (SemEval-2017, PHEME, RumorEval-2019), corresponding to the average thread lengths in these datasets. The experiments were conducted on two Quadro RTX 8000 GPUs, each equipped with 48 GB of VRAM.

Since PHEME contains only partial stance annotations, the model was initially trained on the stance-labeled RumorEval-2019 and SemEval-2017, omitting the stance-based embedding aggregation and the stance label encoding using BiLSTM. Given that these datasets exhibit a strong bias toward the *Comment* stance, we employed SMOTE [21] oversampling technique to balance the stance distribution and enhance model generalization. However, SMOTE was not applied to the rumor verification task to ensure a fair comparison with baseline approaches. The best-performing model from this pretraining stage was subsequently utilized to predict stance labels for PHEME.

D. Evaluation Metrics, Baselines, and Results

Model performance is assessed using macro F1-score and accuracy, with the best-performing model—determined based on validation macro F1-score—selected for final evaluation. All hyperparameters were meticulously fine-tuned using the development dataset, and the reported results are averaged over ten experimental runs. The model is compared against the following rumor detection baselines:

1) **eventAI** [22]: Securing first place in the RumorEval-2019 competition task [23], eventAI leverages multidimensional information and employs an ensemble learning strategy to improve rumor verification performance.
2) **Longformer** [12]: Introduces a fine-tuned Longformer, that is a multi-task learning framework with the bottom part predicting rumor stance and the upper part classifying rumor veracity.

TABLE I
DETAILED STATISTICS OF THE DATASETS.

Dataset	#Threads	#Tweets	Stance Distribution				Rumor Veracity Labels		
			#Support	#Deny	#Query	#Comment	#True	#False	#Unverified
SemEval-17	325	5,568	1,004	415	468	3,685	145	74	106
RumorEval-19	446	8,574	1,184	606	608	6,176	185	138	123
PHEME	2,402	105,354	-	-	-	-	1,067	638	697

3) **Coupled Hierarchical Transformer (CHT)** [24]: This method partitions conversational threads into multiple groups based on their hierarchical structure. Each group is independently processed using BERT to extract contextual features, that are subsequently integrated through a Transformer network for rumor verification.
4) **Joint Rumor and Stance Model (JRSM)** [18]: This approach utilizes a graph transformer to encode input data and a partition filter network to explicitly model rumor-specific, stance-specific, and shared interactive features, that are used for joint rumor and stance classification.
5) **SAMGAT** [25]: This employs Graph Attention Networks (GATs) [26] to model contextual relationships between posts. Although originally designed for binary rumor classification on the PHEME dataset (excluding the *Unverified* class), we adapt and retrain the model for our experimental setting, extending to three-class classification task.

Table II provides a comparative analysis of the performance of the models. The findings demonstrate that our model significantly outperforms the best-competing system, as validated by McNemar's test with a p-value < 0.05. Furthermore, our results exhibit a standard deviation in the range of 0.006–0.02 across all three datasets over the 10 experimental runs, indicating robust and consistent performance.

E. Discussion and Evaluation

We analyze why our approach achieves superior performance in comparison to the listed baselines. *eventAI* leverages ensemble learning but primarily relies on multidimensional handcrafted features, that may not generalize well across datasets. While *Longformer* effectively handles long text sequences, its multi-task learning framework is limited in capturing the structural relationships between stance and rumor veracity. *CHT* processes conversational threads in disjoint hierarchical groups, that disrupts temporal dependencies. *JRSM* treats rumor and stance classification as two separate tasks, but it does not fully exploit the interplay between them. *SAMGAT* relies on GATs to model contextual relationships, but it was originally designed for binary rumor classification and struggles with multi-class settings.

Unlike models such as *CHT*, that process hierarchical groups separately, our aggregation strategy preserves stance distribution and reduces information loss, allowing for better contextual reasoning. Reply posts contain rich contextual signals that indicate how a rumor is perceived within a conversation thread. Simply analyzing the source post alone (as some baselines do) ignores these critical interactions. Our model aggregates reply post embeddings grouped by stance type, ensuring that stance-conditioned representations provide a holistic view of the conversation. Aggregation, in emphasis, also mitigates the sequence length limitation of BERT by summarizing the impact of all replies in a stance-specific manner, preventing the loss of important context and allowing it to dynamically adapt to unseen data rather than relying on predefined feature extraction. Compared to SAMGAT, our model is more adaptable to three-class classification, as demonstrated by the substantial performance boost. Furthermore, while baselines implicitly incorporate stance, our model explicitly embeds and encodes stance labels. BiLSTM preserves the chronological order of stance evolution, that is critical for understanding how rumors develop over time and allowing it to capture stance progression and interactions.

Although only Twitter and Reddit data are used in our experiments, this work can be customized and extended to any social media platform actively engaging in fact-checking and where users participate in the subsequent conversations about a source claim. Therefore, our stance-conditioned modeling for rumor verification can also be generalized to Facebook, Instagram, Threads, etc. This will be incorporated into future work.

F. Ablation Study

To assess the contribution of each component, ablation experiments are conducted using the best-performing model on RumorEval-2017 and RumorEval-2019. The study involves systematically removing specific components and thus coming up with the following derivatives: 1) *-Replies*: Excludes reaction posts R, encoding only the source post p; 2) *-Emb agg*: Discards stance-conditioned embedding aggregation, instead encoding the entire rumor event as a single BERT embedding, constrained by the language model's maximum sequence length; 3) *-Stance-aware*: Omits the sequential modeling of stance labels using BiLSTM. The *Ours-whole* configuration represents the complete model.

Table III presents the results of the ablation study. *-Replies* leads to a significant drop in performance, indicating that contextual signals from replies are crucial for rumor verification, as previously highlighted. *-Emb agg* also results in lower performance. This highlights the importance of stance-conditioned embedding aggregation, that ensures that replies are grouped by stance type rather than processed as isolated inputs. Without aggregation, crucial stance patterns may be lost due to BERT's sequence length limitation, leading to incomplete contextual understanding. *-Stance-aware* furthermore negatively impacts

TABLE II
COMPARISON OF OUR RESULTS WITH BASELINE MODELS.

Model	SemEval-2017		RumorEval-2019		PHEME	
	Macro-F1	Acc	Macro-F1	Acc	Macro-F1	Acc
eventAI	0.618	0.629	0.577	0.591	0.342	0.357
Longformer	0.662	0.673	0.672	0.684	0.452	0.469
CHT	0.680	0.678	0.579	0.611	0.396	0.466
SAMGAT	0.702	0.709	0.542	0.562	0.409	0.418
JRSM	0.754	0.767	0.598	0.623	0.448	0.479
Ours	**0.774**	**0.781**	**0.636**	**0.648**	**0.641**	**0.643**

TABLE III
ABLATION STUDY RESULTS.

Model	RumorEval-2017		RumorEval-2019	
	Macro-F1	Acc	Macro-F1	Acc
-Replies	0.624	0.632	0.540	0.566
-Emb agg	0.642	0.649	0.552	0.579
-Stance-aware	0.647	0.651	0.548	0.564
Ours-whole	**0.774**	**0.781**	**0.636**	**0.648**

performance. This confirms that modeling stance evolution sequentially is beneficial, as stance shifts over time can indicate the credibility of a rumor. The *Ours-whole* configuration, that includes all modules, achieves the highest performance, validating the effectiveness of our stance-conditoned BiLSTM encoding and reply embedding aggregation.

G. Early Detection

Timely detection of rumors can mitigate their widespread dissemination. To assess early detection capabilities, we define detection checkpoints based on the elapsed time, spanning 24 hours, since the initial post. At each checkpoint, only replies accumulated up to that point are considered for model evaluation.

Figure 3 illustrates Macro-F1 and accuracy scores over time for early rumor detection on the SemEval-2017 dataset. Our model consistently outperforms all baselines throughout the 24-hour period, demonstrating superior effectiveness in detecting rumors early. While all models improve as more information becomes available, our model achieves significantly higher Macro-F1 scores early on, starting with an advantage at 4 hours and maintaining superior performance throughout. This suggests that our approach is more responsive to limited initial data, making it highly effective for early-stage rumor identification and particularly valuable in real-world misinformation scenarios where timely intervention is crucial.

H. Illustrative Example: Debunking a False Rumor

We discuss the modeling and debunking of a rumor event shown in Figure 1. The claim has a *False* veracity and a *Support* stance; our model accurately debunked it as *False* rumor. It can be observed from the diagram that more replies in the conversation thread contain *Comment* and *Query* stances. While *Comment* stance entail neutrality of users towards the claim, key insight is that some people who are exposed to a rumor, before deciding its veracity, will take the step of information inquiry to seek more information or express skepticism without specifically asserting whether it is false [13]. Moreover, three out of nine responses in the discourse are a repetition of the claim post, further intensifying doubt in the credibility of the source. These features enhance modeling stance progression and conversational dynamics, presenting cues for our model to discern signals that help in debunking a rumor.

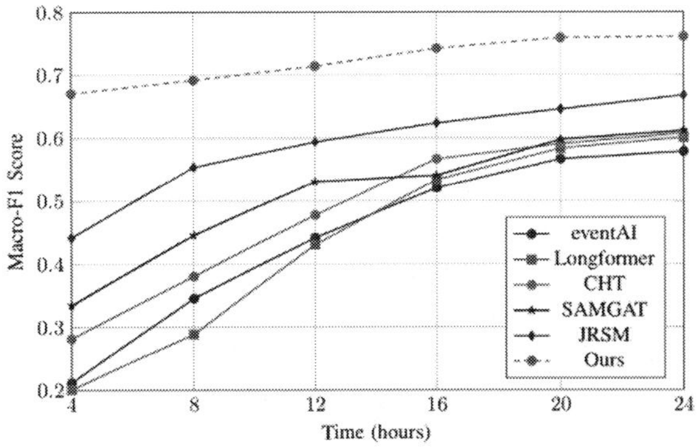

Figure 3. Early Rumor Detection Performance on SemEval-2017.

V. CONCLUSION

This paper presents a novel stance-conditioned rumor verification model that integrates BERT-based source post embeddings and reply post embedding aggregation and BiLSTM encoding of stance labels, to enhance the detection of rumors in online discourse. Our findings highlight several key insights: the explicit incorporation of stance information significantly improves rumor verification, demonstrating that user reactions provide crucial contextual cues; processing stance sequences chronologically using BiLSTM preserves the natural evolution of discussions, leading to more context-aware representations; and leveraging stance-conditioned embedding aggregation mitigates the sequence length limitations of transformer-based models, ensuring a more comprehensive understanding of conversational dynamics. Early rumor detection analysis demonstrates that our model achieves faster and more accurate misinformation detection than competing methods, underscoring its practical utility in real-world misinformation detection.

While the model has shown success, its limitations include a heavy reliance on accurate stance annotations—which might not be consistently available—and training on datasets that may not fully represent real-world misinformation trends across diverse social media platforms. Additionally, the focus on textual content ignores the visual aspects (such as images, memes, and videos) that often accompany online rumors. Future work could reduce dependence on manually labeled data through weakly supervised and self-supervised learning, improve generalization via cross-platform adaptation, incorporate multi-modal data, and further explore extra structural dynamics like stance distribution, hierarchical level encoding, and attention mechanisms.

While the work has positive implications, ethical challenges and risks persist. False negatives and false positives could respectively suppress credible information or allow misinformation to spread, so human validation of predictions is recommended. The system's success could also enable misuse, such as censorship or targeting, requiring transparent deployment and strict ethical guidelines. Additionally, training data biases might lead to unfair outcomes; hence, evaluating and mitigating these biases is critical.

ACKNOWLEDGMENT

This work was supported by the National Science Foundation (NSF) under Award number OIA-1946391, Data Analytics that are Robust and Trusted (DART).

REFERENCES

[1] H. Gong, M. Zhang, Q. Liu, S. Wu, and L. Wang, "Breaking event rumor detection via stance-separated multi-agent debate", *arXiv preprint arXiv:2412.04859*, 2024.

[2] G. Gorrell *et al.*, "SemEval-2019 task 7: RumourEval, determining rumour veracity and support for rumours", in *Proceedings of the 13th International Workshop on Semantic Evaluation*, J. May *et al.*, Eds., Minneapolis, Minnesota, USA: Association for Computational Linguistics, Jun. 2019, pp. 845–854. DOI: 10.18653/v1/S19-2147.

[3] A. Gupta, R. Kumar, and P. Sharma, "Rumor detection in online conversations using transformer-based language models", *Journal of Artificial Intelligence Research*, vol. 68, pp. 1023–1045, 2023.

[4] Y. Li, W. Zhang, and M. Chen, "Leveraging stance detection for improved rumor verification in social media", *ACM Transactions on Knowledge Discovery from Data*, vol. 16, no. 5, pp. 45–67, 2022.

[5] A. Graves and J. Schmidhuber, "Framewise phoneme classification with bidirectional LSTM and other neural network architectures", *Neural Networks*, vol. 18, no. 5-6, pp. 602–610, 2005. DOI: 10.1016/j.neunet.2005.06.042.

[6] J. Devlin, M.-W. Chang, K. Lee, and K. Toutanova, *Bert: Pre-training of deep bidirectional transformers for language understanding*, 2019. arXiv: 1810.04805 [cs.CL].

[7] J. Khoo, D. Wu, and L. Tan, "Conversational context and rumor propagation: A neural approach", in *Proceedings of the Conference on Empirical Methods in Natural Language Processing (EMNLP)*, 2023, pp. 2123–2135.

[8] K. Shu, A. Sliva, and S. Wang, "Fake news and misinformation: A deep learning perspective", *IEEE Transactions on Computational Social Systems*, vol. 8, no. 3, pp. 556–573, 2021.

[9] R. Yang, J. Ma, H. Lin, and W. Gao, "A weakly supervised propagation model for rumor verification and stance detection with multiple instance learning", *arXiv preprint arXiv:2204.02626*, 2022.

[10] Q. Mai, S. Gauch, D. Adams, and M. Huang, *Sequence graph network for online debate analysis*, 2024. arXiv: 2406.18696 [cs.CL].

[11] S. Jami *et al.*, "Rumor stance classification in online social networks: The state-of-the-art, prospects, and future challenges", *arXiv preprint arXiv:2208.01721*, 2022.

[12] A. Khandelwal, "Fine-tune longformer for jointly predicting rumor stance and veracity", *arXiv preprint arXiv:2007.07803*, 2020.

[13] Z. Zhao, P. Resnick, and Q. Mei, "Enquiring minds: Early detection of rumors in social media from enquiry posts", in *Proceedings of the 24th international conference on world wide web*, 2015, pp. 1395–1405.

[14] P. Jia *et al.*, "An improved bilstm approach for user stance detection based on external commonsense knowledge and environment information", *Applied Sciences*, vol. 12, no. 21, p. 10 968, 2022.

[15] L. Derczynski *et al.*, "Semeval-2017 task 8: Rumoureval: Determining rumour veracity and support for rumours", *arXiv preprint arXiv:1704.05972*, 2017.

[16] A. Zubiaga, M. Liakata, and R. Procter, "Learning reporting dynamics during breaking news for rumour detection in social media", *arXiv preprint arXiv:1610.07363*, 2016.

[17] B. Han and T. Baldwin, "Lexical normalisation of short text messages: Makn sens a# twitter", in *Proceedings of the 49th annual meeting of the association for computational linguistics: Human language technologies*, 2011, pp. 368–378.

[18] N. Luo *et al.*, "Joint rumour and stance identification based on semantic and structural information in social networks", *Applied Intelligence*, vol. 54, no. 1, pp. 264–282, 2024.

[19] Y. Liu *et al.*, "Roberta: A robustly optimized bert pretraining approach", in *arXiv preprint arXiv:1907.11692*, 2019.

[20] D. P. Kingma and J. Ba, "Adam: A method for stochastic optimization", *International Conference on Learning Representations (ICLR)*, 2015. arXiv: 1412.6980 [cs.LG].

[21] N. V. Chawla, K. W. Bowyer, L. O. Hall, and W. P. Kegelmeyer, "Smote: Synthetic minority over-sampling technique", *Journal of artificial intelligence research*, vol. 16, pp. 321–357, 2002.

[22] Q. Li, Q. Zhang, and L. Si, "EventAI at SemEval-2019 task 7: Rumor detection on social media by exploiting content, user credibility and propagation information", in *Proceedings of the 13th International Workshop on Semantic Evaluation*, J. May *et al.*, Eds., Minneapolis, Minnesota, USA: Association for Computational Linguistics, Jun. 2019, pp. 855–859. DOI: 10.18653/v1/S19-2148.

[23] G. Gorrell *et al.*, "Rumoureval 2019: Determining rumour veracity and support for rumours", *arXiv preprint arXiv:1809.06683*, 2018.

[24] J. Yu, J. Jiang, L. M. S. Khoo, H. L. Chieu, and R. Xia, "Coupled hierarchical transformer for stance-aware rumor verification in social media conversations", Association for Computational Linguistics, 2020.

[25] Y. Li, Z. Chu, C. Jia, and B. Zu, "Samgat: Structure-aware multilevel graph attention networks for automatic rumor detection", *PeerJ Computer Science*, vol. 10, e2200, 2024.

[26] P. Veličković *et al.*, "Graph attention networks", in *International Conference on Learning Representations (ICLR)*, 2018.

Defect Prevention Review by Process Relationship Matrix

Shuichiro Yamamoto
Information Engineering, IPUT in Nagoya
Nagoya, Japan
e-mail: yamamoto.shu@n.iput.ac.jp

***Abstract*—To clarify business process completeness, we proposed a business process diagram that describes six aspects: input, output, accepting conditions, resource conditions, exception conditions, and judgement conditions. By separating exception conditions from the output, the proposed diagram has the advantage of making it possible to detect and respond to defects and extract exception handling knowledge. The procedure for reviewing the diagram has not been specified. In this paper, we define a process relationship matrix to demonstrate a step-by-step review procedure for preventing defects in business process diagrams. The main output of the paper is the business process review method using a process relationship matrix.**

Keywords-business process; knowledge management; defect prevention; review; process relationship matrix.

I. INTRODUCTION

Ji Koutei Kanketsu (JKK) [1] in Japanese is a word that translates to self (Ji), process (Koutei), and completion (Kanketsu). Self-process completion (JKK) is a method that optimizes the entire production process, not just a specific process.

To introduce JKK, it is necessary to define not only business procedures that define the flow of work, but also requirements organization sheets that define business requirements. The requirements organization sheet consists of fields for the necessary items/information, business inputs, and business outputs for each business process. The necessary item and information field clarifies the input, tools, methods, capabilities/authority, and reasons as conditions for the quality of product. The input field describes the receiving criteria, such as when, where, and what. The output field describes where to sink, by when, and what to produce. The judgment criteria field describes the criteria to judge that "output of the process is good."

JKK clarifies the completeness conditions for each business process element. The requirement organizing sheet is an essential characteristic of JKK.

Salvadorinhoa and Teixeira [2] pointed that Business Process Model can not only help organizations improve their Industry 4.0 environment, but also facilitate knowledge acquisition and distribution. As long as the digitalization of business is promoted, business process documentation become vital for business process continuity. The digitalization re-construct the traditional business process into a new digitalized business process [3]. For example, Digital Balanced Scorecard (DBSC) [4] consists of the digital business process.

Leonard and Swap [5] defined deep smarts as expertise that allows experts to instantly grasp complex situations and make fast and wise decisions to address real-world problems. In other words, deep smarts are "powerful expertise formed beliefs and social influences that can generate insights based on tacit knowledge derived from direct experience." For example, in production process design, a challenge is how to transfer defect investigation knowledge from an expert to a novice. An example of deep smarts is the knowledge of fault investigation held by an experienced engineer.

The business process completeness diagram proposed by Yamamoto and Fujimoto [6] is a diagram whose elements are hexagonal nodes with six vertices. The vertices have six sides: input, output, receiving conditions, resource conditions, exception conditions, and decision conditions. The receiving, input, resource, and decision sides represent the outside-in flow from external elements. The output and exception sides represent the inside-out flow to external elements. A distinctive feature of the defect prevention diagram is that exceptions and outputs are separated by separate arrows.

In this paper, we renamed the business completeness diagram as the defect prevention diagram, because business completeness is achieved by preventing defects in business processes.

In the following, we propose a procedure for creating a defect prevention diagram and a review method in Section II. Furthermore, we explain an example of application in Section III. We provide a discussion in Section IV, and conclude in Section V.

II. BUSINESS PROCESS DESIGN APPROACH

A defect prevention diagram consists of business processes and flow relationships between business processes. In a business process, input, output, receiving conditions, resource conditions, judgment conditions, and exception conditions are clarified. Flow relationships include flows from output to input and flows from exception conditions to input, resource conditions, and judgment conditions.

The Input describes the trigger and information for starting an action. The Output describes the response and information as a result of the action. Accepting conditions describe the conditions for executing an action. Resource conditions describe the people, equipment, information, and activities required to output the action results. Judgment conditions describe the criteria for outputting the action results. Exception conditions describe the conditions under which output cannot be generated because the receiving conditions, resource conditions, and judgment conditions are not met.

Figure 1 shows the defect prevention diagram process element.

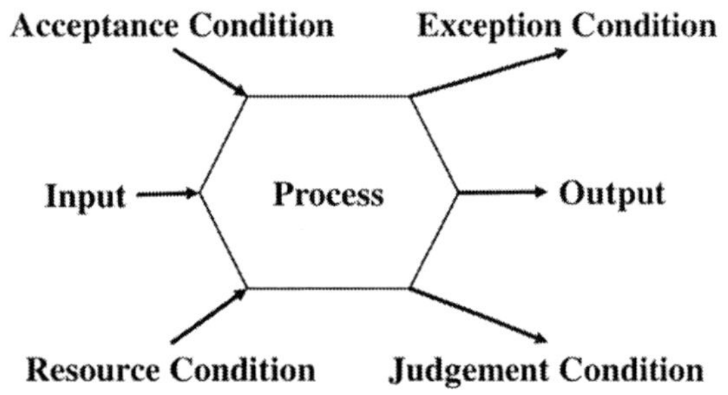

Figure 1. Defect prevention diagram process.

A. *Defect Prevention Diagram Creation*

The step-by-step procedure for creating a defect prevention diagram is shown below.

[Step 1] Identify the business process and name the business action.

[Step 2] For the business process, connect a flow relationship from the output of the preceding business to the input of the succeeding business. At this time, the input and output for the business process are named.

[Step 3] For the business process, identify the receiving conditions, resource conditions, and judgment conditions. For cases where these conditions are not met, extract the exception conditions.

[Step 4] Add an exception flow that connects the extracted exception conditions to the input conditions of the appropriate business process. At this time, if there is no business process to connect the exception flow to, add a new business process to the defect prevention diagram. Also, find the input that will be the output destination of the added business process, and add a flow relationship to the corresponding business process.

[Step 5] Check that the created defect prevention diagram is appropriate from the following perspectives.

- There are no missing business processes
- There are no missing inputs and outputs
- There are no missing conditions
- There are no missing exceptions
- There are no missing flow relationships

[Step 6] If there are any missing conditions in step 5, repeat the corresponding step. Otherwise, end.

(End of procedure)

B. *Business relationship analysis*

For the business process set P that constitutes the defect prevention diagram D, the business process relationship matrix M can be defined as follows.

TABLE I. BUSINESS PROCESS RELATIONSHIP MATRIX

	X	Y
X	Goal of X	X to S: Y Relationship
Y	Y to T: X Relationship	Goal of Y

In Table I, S and T are either the receiving condition A, the resource condition R, or the judgment condition J. If S and T are omitted, they are taken to be the relationship to the input of the target process.

The diagonal element M (X, X) describes the purpose of business process X. The off-diagonal element M (X, Y) describes the connection flow from business process X to either the input, receiving condition, resource condition, or judgment condition of Y.

The business process relationship matrix can be used to comprehensively check the connection flow between business processes that make up the defect prevention diagram. For example, the transitive closure of the business process relationship matrix can define a set of connection relationships for business processes. The set of connection relationships for X in Table I is $\Sigma_{k=1,n} (R_{xy} \cdot R_{yx})^k$. R_{xy} is the relationship from X to S: Y, and R_{yx} is the relationship from Y to T:X.

Similarly, the set of connection relationships for Y in Table I is $\Sigma_{k=1,n} (Ryx \cdot Rxy)^k$.

The process relationship matrix is used to identify defects caused by the flow relationship among processes.

The scalability of the matrix approach depends on the complexity of the number of relations between processes. The approach can be adaptable for any business process relationships by using matrix representation.

C. *Process Checklist*

The process review list is defined as issues of concern for six aspects, as follows.

[Process name]
[Input] issues on input labels
[Accepting condition] issues on accepting arrow labels
[Resource condition] issues on resource arrow labels
[Judgement condition] issues on judgement arrow labels
[Output] issues on output arrow labels
[Exception condition] issues on exception arrow labels

By using the checklist, defects on the process aspect can be derived.

III. CASE STUDY

The Shinkansen bogie crack trouble is said to be a problem of the entire system [7]. If we consider the Shinkansen bogie crack trouble as a system, the main components are (1) the cracked bogie, (2) the maintenance staff who confirmed the bogie abnormality, (3) the control person who ordered the bogie inspection, and (4) the supervisor who manages the overall train management process.

The Shinkansen express goes from Okayama to Tokyo, through Shin-Osaka, and Nagoya. The maintenance staff who boarded the train at Okayama Station confirmed the abnormal sound and suggested to the dispatcher by phone that the bogie be inspected at Shin-Osaka Station. At this time, the control person was receiving an inquiry from the supervisor and did not hear this suggestion from maintenance staff. As a result, the Shinkansen continued to run until JR Central decided to stop it at Nagoya Station.

This train operation management process includes the process in which the maintenance staff confirms the bogie abnormality, the process in which the maintenance staff proposes to inspect the bogie and asks the dispatcher for a decision, and the process in which the dispatcher responds to the inquiry from the dispatcher.

The inspection proposal from the maintenance staff conflicted with the inquiry from the dispatcher, resulting in a loss of information in that the dispatcher did not hear the inspection proposal. This train operation managing process includes supervision, command, problem detection, and train inspection processes, as shown in Figure 2.

As shown in the Table II, inputs for the control process include status inquiries, inspection requests, and inspection reports, and it is clear that there is a possibility that these may conflict. For this reason, it is necessary to prevent inputs from being lost when there is conflict by prioritizing the conditions for receiving these inputs.

In addition, outputs include status reports and inspection instructions, and it is clear that there is a possibility that these outputs may conflict. In this case, it is necessary to avoid output conflicts by specifying the judgment conditions.

TABLE II. PROCESS RELATIONSHIP MATRIX FOR TRAIN MANAGEMENT

	Supervise	Control	Detect	Inspect
Supervise	Governance	Status inquiry		
Control	Status report	Command and Control		Inspection instructions
Detect		Inspection request	Check for abnormalities	
Inspect		Inspection report		Inspection

This consideration is also clarified in the following checklist for the control process.

The Process Checklist for command process is as follows.

[Process name] Command process

[Input] Status inquiry, inspection request, inspection report

[Accepting conditions] Are there any conflicts between status inquiry, inspection request, and inspection report?

[Resource conditions] Commander, command procedure

[Judgment conditions] Are there any conflicts between reports and inspection instructions?

[Output] Status report, inspection instructions

[Exception conditions] Who should be notified of command exceptions?

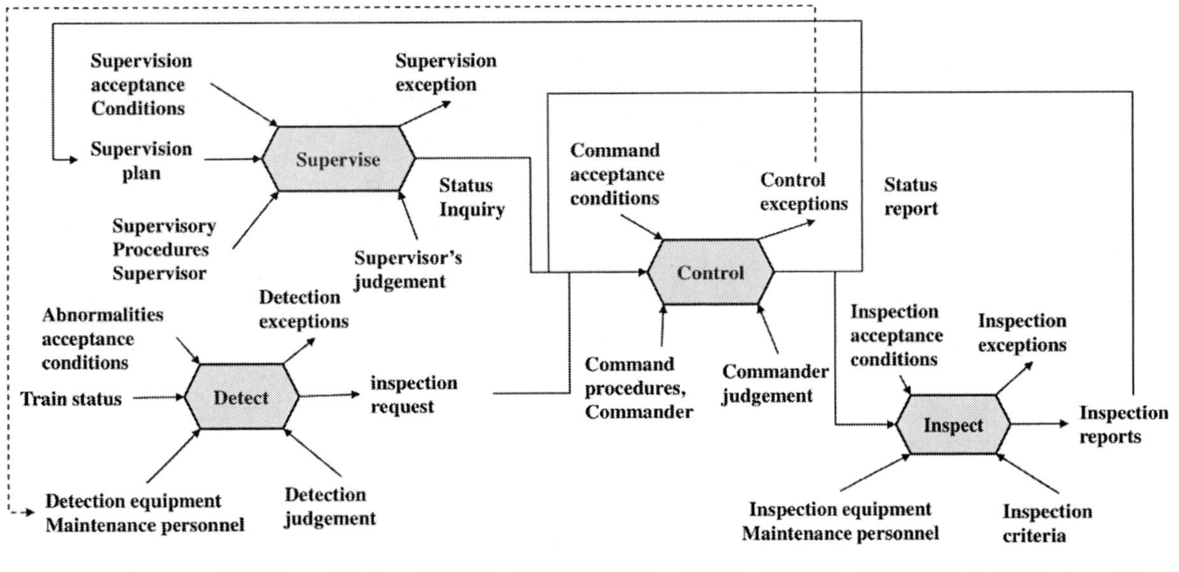

Figure 2. Train operation management process.

IV. Discussion

A. Novelty

In this paper, we proposed a procedure for creating defect prevention diagrams and a review method.

In a defect prevention diagram, business process knowledge can be organized hierarchically using L1: business process knowledge, L2: business flow-related knowledge, L3: business process action condition knowledge, and L4: business action condition execution knowledge. Here, L1, L2, and L3 can be described in a defect prevention diagram. However, for L4, the described conditions must be evaluated when the actual business process is executed.

In the business process knowledge of a defect prevention diagram, L1 can grasp the overall picture of the business process by identifying the necessary actions that make up the business process. Business flow-related knowledge L2 can recognize the dependencies between business processes. Business process action condition knowledge L3 can recognize what conditions are necessary to execute the business. The difference between L3 and L4 is the difference between knowing the conditions and being able to appropriately confirm and evaluate those conditions. Condition evaluation knowledge L4 should be specified so that the evaluation results do not vary depending on the individual for the same conditions.

In the defect prevention diagram, this type of business process knowledge classification is used to organize business knowledge that has traditionally been thought to vary between individuals, making it possible to clarify where the variations in knowledge are occurring.

B. Applicability

In this paper, we confirmed the applicability of the proposed method by applying it to train operation monitoring operations. Because this case is an important business process in fields other than operation monitoring operations, the proposed method may be applicable to a wider range of applicable business processes.

C. Comparison with Root cause analysis

In Root Cause Analysis (RCA), when a defect is detected in a system, the cause of the defect is identified. Once the cause is identified, measures are devised to prevent the defect from occurring in the system.

In contrast, in defect prevention analysis, which is the premise of the defect prevention diagram, the success conditions and exceptions of the system are first defined. Next, measures to deal with exceptions are devised in the system. Defects that occur during the operation of the system are identified and the planned measures are implemented.

D. Limitation

In this paper, we proposed a method for reviewing defect prevention diagrams. However, we have only applied it to one case study. In the future, we need to quantitatively evaluate the effectiveness of the method by applying it to many cases.

V. Conclusion and Future work

In this paper, we proposed a procedure for creating a defect prevention diagram and a review method. The business process review checklist can validate the completeness of each of the six aspects of the process that constitute the defect prevention diagram. In particular, it can detect conflicts between multiple inputs and outputs. In addition, the process relationship matrix can analyze the comprehensive dependencies between the business processes that constitute the defect prevention diagram.

By defining transition relationships based on the elements of the business relationship matrix M, it is possible to iteratively track influence relations. In other words, it is possible to define a language expression L of the defect prevention diagram using M. Since it is believed that the equivalence of the defect prevention diagram can be formulated using this L, it is possible to minimize the defect prevention diagram.

Since the defect prevention diagram can complement the response to exceptions in the business process, it is possible to define a business process that can respond to defects as exceptions.

In this paper, the completeness of the defect prevention diagram is formulated by its ability to respond to exceptions. However, we have not yet discussed whether such an exception response is sufficient. Therefore, we plan to continue to consider the completeness of the defect prevention diagram. Moreover, more case studies and technical details shall be provided as future work.

References

[1] S. Sasaki, "Self-process completion - Quality is built in the process," JSQC selection, Japan Society for Quality Control, 2014 (in Japanese).

[2] J. Salvadorinhoa and L. Teixeira, "Organizational knowledge in the I4.0 using BPMN: a case study," CENTERIS2021, Procedia Computer Science 181, pp. 981–988, 2021.

[3] P. Faraboschi, E. Frachetenberg, P. Laplante, D. Milojicic, and R. Saracco, "Digital Transformation: Lights and Shadows," IEEE Computer, pp. 123-130, Apr. 2023.

[4] S. Yamamoto, "A Strategic Map for Digital Transformation," KES 2020, Procedia Computer Science, vol. 176, 2020, pp. 1374-1381.

[5] S. Yamamoto, Business Process Completeness, eKNOW 2024, pp. 24-28.

[6] D. Leonard, and W. Swap, Deep Smarts: How to Cultivate and Transfer Enduring Business Wisdom, Harvard Business Review Press, 2005.Serendipity" The Sixth International Conference on Advances in Computer-Human Interactions (ACHI 2013) IARIA, Feb. 2013, pp. 7-12, ISSN: 2308-4138, ISBN: 978-1-61208-250-9.

[7] Nihon Keizai Shimbun (a Japanese newspaper), Online Edition, Cracks in Shinkansen bogies, discrepancy in recognition of vehicle abnormality, JR West President's press conference, 2017.12.27 (in Japanese).

Measuring Tacit Knowledge Hiding in IT Consulting Firms

Jason Triche
University of Montana
Missoula, MT, USA
email: jason.triche@umontana.edu

Abstract—**Organizations like Information Technology (IT) consulting firms use knowledge as one of their core competencies to gain a competitive edge in the market. These firms rely on the tacit knowledge of their employees to gain a competitive edge in the industry. These highly competitive work environments lend themselves to individuals hiding knowledge from each other for a myriad of reasons, including helping individuals maintain a competitive edge within the firm. Knowledge Hiding (KH), the deliberate hiding of knowledge when asked, has negative effects on organizations. This research explores if tacit knowledge is being deliberately hidden from others when prompted due to this highly competitive work environment. Using social exchange theory and an experimental design method, this research proposes to ask individuals working in the IT consulting sector if they would hide different types of knowledge (tacit vs. explicit) given the competitiveness of the work environment. This research also proposes testing different mediating effects like task interdependence and professional commitment to reduce tacit knowledge hiding in IT consulting firms.**

Keywords-tacit knowledge; knowledge hiding; competitive work environment.

I. INTRODUCTION

The motivation for this research comes from working in a highly competitive work environment in the field of Information Technology (IT) consulting. A core competency of consulting companies is the tacit knowledge (i.e., skills, ideas, and experiences that are hard to codify) and explicit knowledge (i.e., information that is easy to share, document, and understand) gained and created by working with multiple clients over multiple industries and documenting best practices, common pitfalls, and lessons learned. IT consulting companies also create a highly competitive work environment where employees compete against each other for promotions and merit increases. The highly competitive work environment fosters team productivity and organizational gains but results in employees hiding knowledge from each other to maintain a competitive edge for themselves. Literature has shown that the organization is negatively impacted when employees hide knowledge from each other. Scant research exists examining tacit knowledge hiding in highly competitive work environments. Based on a literature search, there appears only one article that examines tacit and explicit KH in a highly competitive work environment, specifically in the field of academics [1]. Presumably, the field of academics has a different promotion and tenure process than the private sector and may lead to different degrees of hiding tacit knowledge. Hence, studying other highly competitive work environments (e.g., IT consulting) is important. This leads to the following research questions. 1) Is tacit knowledge hidden more than explicit knowledge in these environments? and, 2) Are there ways to encourage employees not to hide tacit knowledge from each other while maintaining the organization's competitive environment?

There are both practical and theoretical contributions to this research. Findings from this research can help fill the gap in tacit knowledge hiding in a competitive work environment. Finding ways to ameliorate the negative effects of tacit knowledge hiding can help organizations that foster a competitive work environment.

Relevant literature on knowledge hiding, tacit vs. explicit knowledge, and highly competitive work environments are discussed in Section II. Section III provides a proposed methodology that examines tacit knowledge hiding for workers in a highly competitive working environment. Next steps and future work are discussed in Section IV.

II. LITERATURE REVIEW

Knowledge Hiding (KH) is defined as "an intentional attempt by an individual to withhold or conceal knowledge that has been requested by another person" [2. p 65]. KH is unique given that a knowledge seeker (i.e., an individual seeking knowledge) must request knowledge from another individual, and that individual must intentionally hide knowledge, thus being referred to as the knowledge hider. KH is a unique construct that is different from other types of knowledge-related behaviors, such as knowledge sharing or knowledge hoarding. KH can take place at the individual level, the team level, and the organizational level. According to [2], KH consists of three dimensions: playing dumb (the knowledge hider pretends not to know the knowledge that is being requested), rationalized hiding (the knowledge hider provides reasons for not revealing the knowledge), and evasive hiding (the knowledge hider offers wrong or incomplete information).

A competitive work environment, like most IT consulting firms, is a workplace culture where employees are motivated to outperform their peers, often driven by the desire to secure rewards and recognition [3]. Competitive environments often foster a climate where employees are more likely to engage in knowledge hiding to protect their own interests and maintain a competitive edge. A competitive psychological climate can exacerbate knowledge hiding, as employees may feel threatened and resort to self-protective behaviors [4]. This is particularly evident in performance-oriented climates where employees' actions are compared against their peers [5].

Tacit knowledge refers to knowledge that is difficult to communicate or convey in words. It is often gained through personal experience, context, and practice, making it inherently subjective and context-specific. Conversely, explicit knowledge can be easily communicated, documented, and shared. Research has shown that tacit knowledge can enhance firm performance, particularly in consulting firms where individual expertise and insights are crucial. Consulting firms can leverage tacit knowledge to improve decision-making, foster collaboration, and drive innovation, ultimately leading to better client outcomes and competitive advantage [6].

Given the difficulty of documenting and sharing tacit knowledge, and given that tacit knowledge is crucial for the success of consulting firms, and consulting firms operate in a highly competitive environment where knowledge hiding is heightened, is tacit knowledge hiding more prevalent than explicit knowledge hiding in a competitive work environment? If so, are there ways for consulting firms to overcome hiding this valuable tacit knowledge?

III. METHODS

The nature of the construct makes it hard to measure since KH involves specifically asking for information from an individual and not receiving it. Much of the research in this area involves using a survey instrument. A few studies use semi-structured interviews or an experimental design [7].

In this research, the researchers propose using a 2 x 2 experimental design to ask the participants (i.e., potential knowledge hiders) working in IT consulting to share either tacit or explicit knowledge in a competitive or non-competitive work environment. The researchers will manipulate the types of knowledge and the competitiveness of the environment and then ask the participants to score their willingness to share that knowledge with the requestor (i.e., knowledge seeker). An experiment, compared to a survey, could decrease the reluctance to admit to knowledge hiding since the scenarios are fictitious, and they are not asking what the participants have done in the past.

The researchers will use existing measurements of tacit and explicit knowledge [8] and competitive work environments [2] to guide the development of scenarios for the experiment. For example, one scenario would prime the participant into a competitive work environment by stating that promotions at this company are based on high expectations of individual success, and those not promoted to the next level will be coached to find another company that is a better fit. A pilot study will be used to verify that the scenarios meet face validity and are reliable before circulating the instrument to a larger sample of IT consulting professionals. IT professionals will be recruited through existing contacts at IT consulting firms like Accenture, E&Y, KMPG, and Slalom Consulting.

In this same research stream, the researchers would like to understand what the organization can do to reduce the hiding of valuable tacit knowledge. Reference [1] examined tacit and explicit knowledge hiding in academia, which is also considered a competitive work environment. They found that task interdependence and social support moderated explicit KH, but not tacit KH. This research aims to investigate whether this also holds true in IT consulting, where tacit knowledge may be more beneficial to the organization compared to an academic setting. This manipulation can be a part of the original experiment based on the participants' dependent variable response (i.e., willingness to share).

IV. CONCLUSION AND FUTURE WORK

This research aims to study valuable tacit knowledge using social exchange theory in IT consulting firms to 1) determine that it is indeed being hidden and 2) verify if researched antecedents work in this context using an experimental design. The results from this research could help expose the estimated extent of tacit knowledge hiding in IT consulting firms. Depending on the results of this research, the findings could also assist managers in IT consulting firms in finding ways to reduce the tacit knowledge hiding problem.

REFERENCES

[1] T. Hernaus, M. Černe, C. E. Connelly, N. Pološki Vokić, and M. Škerlavaj, "Evasive knowledge hiding in academia: when competitive individuals are asked to collaborate," Journal of Knowledge Management, vol. 23, no. 4, pp. 597–618, 2019.

[2] C. E. Connelly, D. Zweig, J. Webster, and J. P. Trougakos, "Knowledge hiding in organizations," Journal of Organizational Behavior, vol. 33, no. 1, pp. 64-88, 2012.

[3] S. Sajeva, "Encouraging knowledge sharing among employees: how reward matters," Procedia-Social and Behavioral Sciences, vol. 156, pp. 130-134, 2014.

[4] M. S. Han, K. Masood, D. Cudjoe, and Y. Wang, "Knowledge hiding as the dark side of competitive psychological climate," Leadership & Organization Development Journal, vol. 42, no. 2, pp. 195–207, 2020.

[5] Y. Sofyan, E. De Clercq, and Y. Shang, "Does intraorganizational competition prompt or hinder performance? The risks for proactive employees who hide knowledge," Personnel Review, vol. 52, no. 3, pp. 777–798, 2022.

[6] I. Yazici et al., "A comparative analysis of machine learning techniques and fuzzy analytic hierarchy process to determine the tacit knowledge criteria," Annals of Operations Research, vol. 308, no. 1-2, pp. 753-776, 2020.

[7] A. Anand, F. Offergelt, and P. Anand, "Knowledge hiding – a systematic review and research agenda," Journal of Knowledge Management, vol. 26, no. 6, pp. 1438–1457, 2021.

[8] N. Leonard and G. S. Insch, "Tacit Knowledge in Academia: A Proposed Model and Measurement Scale," The Journal of Pschology, vol. 139, no. 6, pp. 496-512, 2005.

Fair Learning for Bias Mitigation and Quality Optimization in Paper Recommendation

Uttamasha Anjally Oyshi, Susan Gauch
Department of Electrical Engineering & Computer Science
University of Arkansas
Fayetteville, USA
e-mails: {uoyshi, sgauch}@uark.edu

Abstract—**Despite frequent double-blind review, demographic biases of authors still disadvantage the underrepresented groups. We present Fair-PaperRec, a MultiLayer Perceptron (MLP) based model that addresses demographic disparities in post-review paper acceptance decisions while maintaining high-quality requirements. Our methodology penalizes demographic disparities while preserving quality through intersectional criteria (e.g., race, country) and a customized fairness loss, in contrast to heuristic approaches. Evaluations using conference data from ACM Special Interest Group on Computer-Human Interaction (SIGCHI), Designing Interactive Systems (DIS), and Intelligent User Interfaces (IUI) indicate a 42.03% increase in underrepresented group participation and a 3.16% improvement in overall utility, indicating that diversity promotion does not compromise academic rigor and supports equity-focused peer review solutions.**

Keywords-Fairness-aware recommendation; Paper selection; Demographic bias mitigation

I. INTRODUCTION

Double-blind review often does not eradicate systemic biases linked to authors' demographics, reputations, or institutional affiliations, despite attempts to ensure impartiality [1]–[4]. Recent data indicates that even the most stringent anonymization techniques can be undermined by analyzing writing style or cross-referencing previous articles [5], [6]. This tendency can sustain biases against particular groups, including women, racial minorities, and researchers from underrepresented areas [3], [7]–[9]. Simultaneously, there is a growing dependence on recommendation algorithms to optimize processes such as paper selection, grant distribution, and significant publication identification [10]–[12]. While these systems can accelerate decision-making, they also pose a danger of perpetuating biases present in the training data, particularly if they focus only on predictive accuracy [13]–[15]. Therefore, it is imperative to devise novel methodologies that explicitly include demographic justice, preventing the perpetuation of historical inequalities.

In this paper, we introduce Fair-PaperRec, a fairness-aware recommendation framework specifically designed to mitigate post-review bias. Unlike previous heuristic-based approaches that often handle single-attribute fairness constraints or overlook intersectionality, in our approach:

- We surpass single-attribute approaches by incorporating multiple demographic attributes (e.g., race, country) and constructing multi-dimensional profiles that capture underlying biases.
- After a double-blind review, a specialized fairness penalty is implemented to address demographic disparities, thereby correcting latent biases without the need to replace existing processes.
- Our method ensures that the quality of the paper is maintained throughout by ensuring demographic parity, thereby obtaining equitable representation without compromising academic rigor.

Our results demonstrate improved representation in the participation of underrepresented groups, as well as an enhancement in overall paper quality, as indicated by the h-index. Notably, these findings reveal that enhanced inclusivity need not diminish academic rigor; a fairness-driven approach can yield greater demographic parity while simultaneously preserving, and at times even *enhancing*, the quality of accepted papers.

By mitigating biases in paper selection, our strategy promotes a richer academic discourse and amplifies the representation of marginalized communities, thereby paving the way toward more equitable, high-quality conferences. The paper includes the folling sections, where in Section 2, we review related work. Section 3 presents the proposed methodology. Section 4 explains our experimental setup and metrics. Section 5 provides results and analysis. Finally, the Section 6 concludes the paper.

II. RELATED WORK

We begin by examining double-blind review and bias in academic paper selection, then explore fairness in recommender systems, and finally discuss recent advancements in neural approaches for fair selection.

A. Double-Blind Review and Bias in Academic Paper Selection

Although double-blind review conceals identities [1]–[3], it often fails to eliminate biases in gender, race,

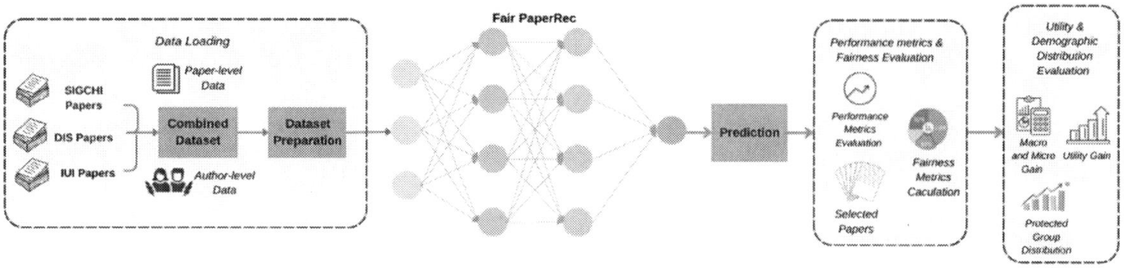

Figure 1. Overview of the Fair-PaperRec Architecture.

or geography [9], [16]. While authorship-attribution can rectify advanced anonymization [5], high-prestige institutions continue to receive favorable reviews [17]. As a result, underrepresented groups, including women and racial minorities, continue to be marginalized [18], and substantial acceptance rate disparities persist [7], [8].

B. Fairness in Recommendation Systems

When optimizing solely for accuracy, recommenders frequently exacerbate biases [11], [19]. Although some fairness issues are addressed by multi-objective [13], adversarial [14], and re-ranking methods [15], the majority of these methods concentrate on single attributes or user-item data, leaving intersectional biases in paper acceptance unaccounted for. In academic settings, *provider fairness* is equivalent to *author fairness*, which protects minority researchers [20]. There are very few algorithms that resolve post-review bias, not to mention, multi-attribute fairness [12], [21].

C. Post-Review Bias Mitigation and Neural Approaches

Some heuristic methods attempt to rebalance accepted papers after reviews [20], but they risk local optima and often fail to consider multi-attribute fairness. Neural-based solutions such as *DeepFair* [11] or *Neural Fair Collaborative Filtering* [22] demonstrate that fairness can align with accuracy, yet they typically target commercial recommendations rather than the nuances of academic peer review. Meanwhile, multi-stakeholder optimization [23], [24] highlights the need for more contextual fairness definitions within scholarly publishing. Although certain approaches (e.g., Bulut et al. [25]) employ text-based features like Term Frequency–Inverse Document Frequency (TF-IDF) to improve relevance, they often disregard the imperative of equity for authors from historically marginalized groups.

III. Methodology

Our approach tackles demographic biases in conference data by employing a simple Multilayer Perceptron (MLP) to enforce fairness post-review. We highlight two fundamental principles: (1) revealing and alleviating biases instead of eliminating them, and (2) implementing a straightforward, yet efficient neural architecture that harmonizes equality and utility.

A. Data Collection and Pre-processing

Real-world datasets—particularly those drawn from academic conference submissions—often contain latent biases that mirror systemic imbalances in the scholarly community (e.g., underrepresentation of certain demographics). We utilize datasets from SIGCHI 2017, DIS 2017, and IUI 2017 [20], which naturally reflect systemic disparities (e.g., skewed demographics). Instead of eliminating such biases, our objective is to *recognize and rectify* them.

We describe the process of collecting and preparing the data used in our experiments. The dataset consists of academic papers submitted to conferences, and we employ a variety of pre-processing steps to ensure the data are suitable for training our model.

TABLE I. DEMOGRAPHIC PARTICIPATION FROM PROTECTED GROUPS IN THREE CONFERENCES.

Conference	Gender (%)	Race (%)	Country (%)
SIGCHI	41.88	6.84	21.94
DIS	65.79	35.09	24.56
IUI	43.75	51.56	39.06
Average	50.47	31.16	28.52

1) Data Description: We gathered detailed information at the paper and author levels, resulting in a robust combined dataset. Every paper record has a title, authors, and a conference designation (1 = IUI, 2 = DIS, 3 = SIGCHI). Author records encompass demographic information (gender, race, nationality, career stage), for detailed analysis. We classify SIGCHI 2017 articles as a standard for high-impact research, whereby *Overall* includes all submissions and *Selected* refers to those identified by our algorithms.

2) Data Pre-processing: Several preprocessing steps were undertaken to prepare the dataset for training:

- *Categorical Encoding:* Gender, Country, and Race are subjected to one-hot encoding. Gender is binary (0 = male, 1 = female), Country is categorized as *developed* or *underdeveloped*, and Race comprises

{White, Asian, Hispanic, Black}, with Hispanic and Black designated as protected groups (Table I).

- *Normalization:* Numerical attributes (e.g., h-index) employ min-max scaling for consistent magnitude.
- *Training and Validation Division:* An 80%/20% stratified division guarantees equitable distribution of labels and protected attributes in both subsets.

B. Problem Definition

This study develops a *fairness-aware paper recommendation system* that ensures demographic parity with respect to authors' race and country, while preserving high academic standards. We frame acceptance decisions as a *recommendation* task, where *conference organizers (users)* seek to select from *530 papers (items)* spanning SIGCHI, DIS, and IUI. Each paper (item) includes an *h-index* for quality, demographic data (race, country), and a conference rating (SIGCHI: 1, DIS: 2, IUI: 3).

Our approach enforces fairness constraints on race and country independently, excluding *gender* due to its relatively balanced distribution (see Table I). By leveraging historical acceptance patterns and explicit diversity goals, the system balances the *need for high-quality research* with the *requirement to address demographic biases* in the final recommendation of papers.

Let D represent the dataset of submitted papers, where each paper $p \in D$ is associated with a set of features X_p (e.g., race, country, h-index) and a target variable y_p indicating acceptance (1) or rejection (0). The *race* attribute R_p and *country* attribute C_p are the protected attributes.

We aim to optimize a predictive model $f : X_p \rightarrow \hat{y}_p$ that minimizes the following objective function:

$$\min_{f} \left(\mathcal{L}(f(X_p), y_p) + \lambda \cdot \mathcal{L}_{\text{fairness}}(f, D)\right) \tag{1}$$

Here, $\mathcal{L}(f(X_p), y_p)$ is the *prediction loss* (e.g., Binary Cross-Entropy Loss), $\mathcal{L}_{\text{fairness}}(f, D)$ is the *fairness loss*, penalizing deviations from demographic parity across race and country and λ is a hyperparameter that balances the trade-off between prediction accuracy and fairness.

C. Demographic Parity

We aim to ensure that the probability of a paper being accepted is independent of the protected attributes:

$$P(\hat{y}_p = 1 \mid R_p = r) = P(\hat{y}_p = 1), \quad \forall r \in \text{Race}$$

$$P(\hat{y}_p = 1 \mid C_p = c) = P(\hat{y}_p = 1), \quad \forall c \in \text{Country}$$

Utilizing these equations ensures that the papers authored by individuals from different races and countries have an equal probability of acceptance.

Algorithm 1. FAIR-PAPERREC LOSS FUNCTION.

Input: Model M, Epochs E, Batch size B, Data D, Protected attributes A, Hyperparameter λ
Output: Trained Model M
Initialize Model M
for each $e \in E$ **do**
  Shuffle Data D
  for each batch $\{(X, Y)\} \in D$ with size B **do**
    Predict $\hat{Y} \leftarrow M(X)$
    Calculate Loss:
      $L_{\text{prediction}} \leftarrow \text{PredictionLoss}(Y, \hat{Y})$
      $L_{\text{fairness}} \leftarrow \text{FairnessLoss}(A, \hat{Y})$
    Calculate Total Loss:
      $L_{\text{total}} \leftarrow \lambda \cdot L_{\text{fairness}} + L_{\text{prediction}}$
    Compute gradients $\nabla L_{\text{total}} \leftarrow \frac{\partial L_{\text{total}}}{\partial M}$
    Update Model parameters: $M \leftarrow M - \alpha \nabla L_{\text{total}}$
  end for
end for

D. Fairness Loss

The fairness loss from the objective function in Equation 1 is constructed to minimize statistical parity differences between the protected and non-protected group:

$$\mathcal{L}_{\text{fairness}} = \left(P(\hat{y}_p = 1 \mid G_{\text{p}}) - P(\hat{y}_p = 1 \mid G_{\text{np}})\right)^2 \tag{2}$$

Here, $P(\hat{y}_p = 1 \mid G_{\text{p}})$ denotes the acceptance probability for the protected group and $P(\hat{y}_p = 1 \mid G_{\text{np}})$ is the acceptance probability for the non-protected group.

E. Combined Fairness Loss

Furthermore, we define a combined fairness loss to minimize statistical parity differences across race and country attributes between the protected and unprotected groups, as shown in Equation 3.

$$\begin{aligned} \mathcal{L}_{\text{fairness}} = {} & W_r \left(\frac{1}{N_r} \sum_{p \in G_r} \hat{y}_p - \frac{1}{N} \sum_{p=1}^{N} \hat{y}_p\right)^2 \\ & + W_c \left(\frac{1}{N_c} \sum_{p \in G_c} \hat{y}_p - \frac{1}{N} \sum_{p=1}^{N} \hat{y}_p\right)^2 \end{aligned} \tag{3}$$

G_{r} and G_{c} denote the race and country groups, respectively. N_r and N_c are the number of papers in each group and weights W_r and W_c reflect group distributions.

F. Total Loss

The total loss is the combination of prediction and fairness losses:

$$\mathcal{L}_{\text{total}} = \mathcal{L}_{\text{prediction}} + \lambda \cdot \mathcal{L}_{\text{fairness}}$$

G. Constraints and Considerations

We assess fairness by training our model separately on *race* and *country*, as well as jointly on both attributes to evaluate selection fairness across multiple dimensions.

TABLE II. GAIN CALCULATIONS FOR COUNTRY AND RACE FEATURES WITH UTILITY GAIN (UG_i).

λ	Country Feature			Race Feature		
	Macro Gain (%)	Micro Gain (%)	UG_i (%)	Macro Gain (%)	Micro Gain (%)	UG_i (%)
1	7.71	8.67	3.16	24.81	31.11	0.35
2	10.77	13.23	1.05	33.54	46.30	1.75
2.5	**12.67**	**22.96**	**1.75**	39.25	54.81	1.40
3	13.60	16.96	0.35	**42.03**	**56.48**	**3.16**
5	14.80	19.97	-0.35	43.04	56.11	-0.70
10	13.86	18.73	2.46	52.91	64.81	-0.70

a) Exclusion of Protected Attributes: Race R_p and country C_p are excluded from the input feature set X_p to mitigate direct bias amplification. To achieve joint fairness, both attributes are omitted during training, preventing the model from learning acceptance outcomes influenced by race or country.

b) Indirect Bias Mitigation: A fairness loss promotes demographic parity, addressing indirect biases associated with features related to race or country. The model maintains neutrality by penalizing selection disparities, even in the absence of protected attributes.

c) Scalability: Our method supports datasets of varying scales and complexities, demonstrating strong performance across various academic fields. This scalability ensures fairness across various use cases.

IV. Model Overview

To achieve demographic parity while preserving quality in paper selection, we present a MLP-based neural network (See Figure 1), explicitly engineered to balance the trade-off between fairness and accuracy. It illustrates the correlations between input features, like author demographic attributes and paper quality, while alleviating biases during selection.

A unique fairness loss function was employed to ensure equity, imposing penalties on the model for substantial differences in selection rates between protected and non-protected groups. This loss function is integrated with the conventional prediction loss to attain a balance between diversity and accuracy; the algorithm is shown in Algorithm 1.

The acceptance probabilities for submitted papers are generated by the MLP, which are subsequently ranked to guarantee that the final selection meets both quality and fairness objectives. By selecting top papers according to these probabilities, we ensure equal representation of authors from both protected and non-protected groups while upholding the requisite standard of academic excellence.

A. Selection Mechanism

The model calculates acceptance probabilities for all submitted papers after training. After calculating acceptance odds, the algorithm ranks candidate papers.

Algorithm 2. FAIRNESS-AWARE PAPER SELECTION MECHANISM.

Input: Dataset D, Model M, Number of Accepted Papers N_a, Total Papers N_t
Output: Selected Papers P_{selected}
Initialize: $P_{\text{selected}} \leftarrow \emptyset$
Step 1: Apply trained model M to the entire dataset D
for each paper $p \in D$ **do**
    Compute acceptance probability: $\hat{y}_p \leftarrow M(p)$
end for
Step 2: Rank all papers p by acceptance probability $\hat{y}_p$
Sort D in descending order of $\hat{y}_p$
Step 3: Select top N_a papers:
    $P_{\text{selected}} \leftarrow \{p \mid \hat{y}_p \geq \hat{y}_{(N_a)}\}$
Step 4: Ensure Fairness Constraints
Return P_{selected}

This rating phase ensures underrepresented groups are represented in final admission decisions. Representing this as a suggestion list preserves the peer-review process and corrects residual biases. Algorithm 2 selects the best papers based on probability, ensuring fairness and preserving the desired number of accepted papers.

- *Prediction Aggregation:* The trained MLP model is applied to the entire dataset to obtain predicted acceptance probabilities $\hat{y}_p$ for each paper.
- *Ranking:* Papers are ranked in descending order based on their predicted probabilities.
- *Selection:* The papers with the highest predicted probabilities are selected for acceptance, ensuring the total number of selected papers matches the required acceptance quota.

Mathematically, the selection process is represented as:

$$\text{Selected Papers} = \left\{p \in D \mid \hat{y}_p \geq \hat{y}_{(N_a)}\right\}$$

Here, $\hat{y}_{(N_a)}$ is the N_a-th highest predicted probability in the set $\{\hat{y}_p \mid p \in D\}$ while N_a is the total number of accepted papers and N_t is the total number of submitted papers, where $N_a \leq N_t$.

This approach ensures that the selection process is both informed by the model's predictions and constrained to uphold demographic parity, fostering an equitable and meritocratic paper selection environment.

V. Evaluation and Experiments

This section presents the experimental evaluation of our proposed Fair-PaperRec model on the chosen datasets. To guide the exploration of fairness and quality in our proposed paper recommendation system, we pose the following research questions:

- *RQ1:* How do fairness constraints affect the overall quality (utility) of recommended papers, as measured by metrics, such as the h-index?
- *RQ2:* Does handling race and country as separate protected attributes differ from treating them jointly in terms of fairness outcomes and selection decisions?

- *RQ3:* How do varying weight assignments to multiple protected attributes (race and country) influence the trade-off between fairness and utility?

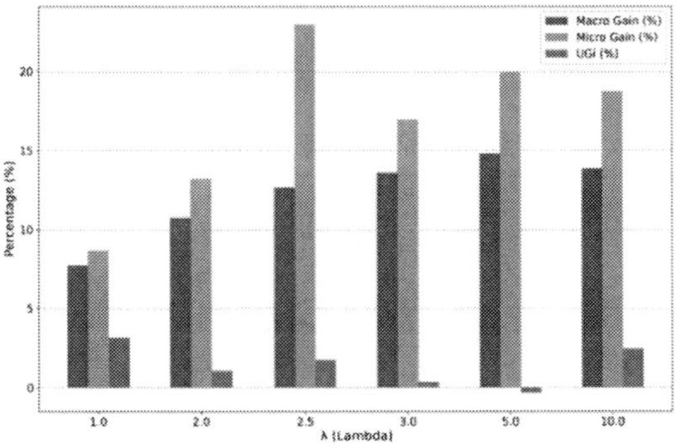

Figure 2. Comparison of Macro and Micro Gains for Country Across Different Fairness Configurations.

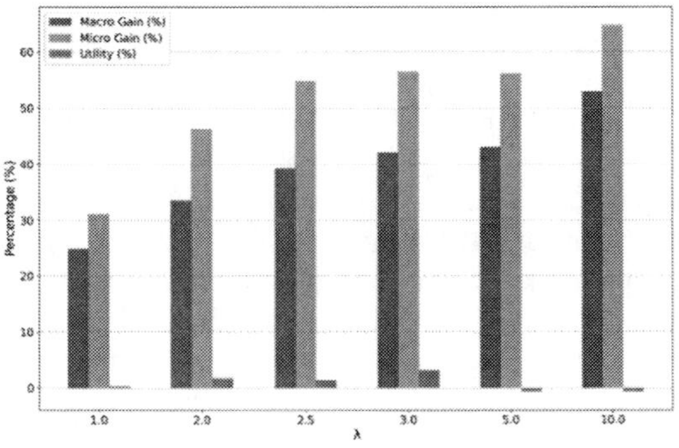

Figure 3. Comparison of Macro and Micro Gains for Race Across Different Fairness Configurations.

A. *Experimental Setting*

We evaluate Fair-PaperRec using datasets from prominent academic conferences, contrasting it with baseline approaches and examining the trade-off between fairness and selection quality. Each experiment is conducted 5 times individually, with *standard deviations* provided for *consistency*.

TABLE III. DISTRIBUTION OF RECOMMENDED PAPERS FROM EACH CONFERENCE.

Label	Country	Race	Multi-Fair
SIGCHI	92.02%	92.00%	92.02%
DIS	4.84%	7.69%	7.40%
IUI	3.14%	0.31%	0.56%
# Papers	351	351	351

1) Implementation Details: All experiments use `PyTorch` on a high-performance machine with two NVIDIA Quadro RTX 4000 Graphics Processing Units (GPUs). Our model is a two-hidden-layer MLP (Rectified Linear Unit (ReLU) activations, Batch Normalization), ending in a sigmoid output for acceptance probabilities. We train for 50 epochs using Adam (learning rate = 0.001), applying early stopping if no improvement occurs over 10 epochs. The fairness regularization parameter λ is tuned to balance utility and demographic parity. Each dataset is split 80/20 (training/validation) via stratified sampling, and each run is repeated five times with different random seeds to average performance metrics and capture variance.

2) Baseline: We compare our model against a baseline Demographic-Blind Model which is a conventional (MLP) model that prioritizes quality and ignores fairness constraints. This model selects the original list of papers chosen by the SIGCHI 2017 program committee.

3) Parameters: A hyperparameter λ is used for controlling the trade-off between prediction accuracy and fairness. Higher values emphasize fairness more strongly.

The weights W_c, W_r respectively denote the weighting factors assigned to the country and race attributes in the fairness loss function, as shown in Equation 3.

B. *Evaluation Metrics*

Diversity is assessed at both the *paper level* and the *author level.* In particular:

- *Macro Gain* represents the percentage increase in the diversity of each feature within the selected papers compared with the baseline, assessing the overall representation of protected groups.
- *Micro Gain* is the percentage increase in the diversity of each feature among authors of the selected papers, providing more detailed perspective on inclusivity.

A *Diversity Gain* [20] further normalizes these macro-level changes (Equation 4), capping each feature at 100 to avoid any single attribute skewing the total. The *F - measure* [20] (Equation 5) then combines this diversity improvement with the resulting utility, offering a harmonic balance between fairness gains and paper quality.

To ensure that enhancements in diversity do not compromise the quality of papers, we assess *Utility Gain* (UG_i). The utility is represented by the weighted h-index corresponding to an author's career stage—Professor, Associate Professor, Lecturer, Post-Doctoral Researcher, or Graduate Student—indicating their distribution within the dataset. Analyzing the values of the h-index in relation to a baseline determines whether equity initiatives compromise academic quality.

$$D_G = \frac{\sum_{i=1}^{n} \min(100, \text{Macro Gain}_{G_i})}{n} \quad (4)$$

$$F = 2 \times \frac{D_G \times (100 - UG_i)}{D_G + (100 - UG_i)} \quad (5)$$

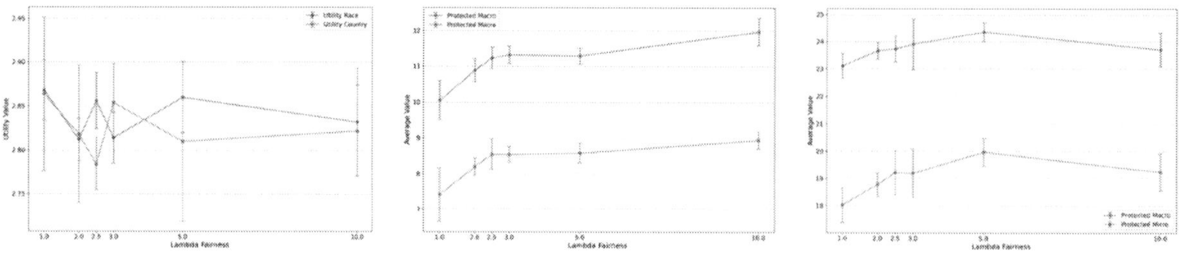

(a) Utility Gain. (b) Macro/Micro for Race. (c) Macro/Micro for Country.

Figure 4. Comparison of gains across different fairness configurations.

C. Interpretation of the Results

The fairness regularization parameter (λ) was evaluated using values from 1 to 10 to examine its impact on fairness, utility, and diversity (see Table II). *RQ1*, which investigates how fairness constraints affect the utility of paper recommendations, was addressed through Figures 2 and 3. For the protected attribute "race," a λ value of 3 achieved an effective balance between diversity (both micro and macro) and utility. For "country," the optimal λ value was 2.5, which performed best across metrics. As λ increased, both micro and macro diversity gain improved, but utility decreased, indicating a reduction in the quality of recommended papers. This observation highlights the trade-off between increasing fairness and maintaining high utility, providing a clear answer to *RQ1*.

The varying optimal λ values for race and country reflect the different disparity ratios between these protected groups. This directly addresses *RQ2*, which examines how independent consideration of race and country affects fairness outcomes. The higher disparity ratio for race, which results from the smaller fraction of protected racial groups in the initial pool, requires a higher λ to achieve a balance between fairness and utility compared to country. Adjusting λ based on the specific levels of disparity in each protected group is essential to achieving optimal results. Overall, fairness interventions led to positive diversity outcomes in both micro and macro measures compared to the baseline, indicating the benefit of targeted fairness constraints.

Figure 4 presents three comparisons: (a) Utility Gain, (b) Race Fairness, and (c) Country Fairness, providing insights into utility values and diversity indicators across various λ values. The first graph shows that utility remained relatively stable for race but fluctuated significantly for country, especially at higher λ values, with larger error bars indicating greater uncertainty. Utility tended to decrease for both attributes as λ increased, further emphasizing the trade-off between fairness and utility discussed in *RQ1*.

The second and third graphs, which illustrate the protected macro and micro diversity measures for race and country, reveal that increasing λ consistently improved macro diversity for both attributes, with race showing more steady growth. In contrast, micro diversity measures, particularly for country, displayed more variability and less predictable improvement. These results suggest that macro diversity benefits are easier to achieve under higher fairness constraints, while micro-level improvements, especially for country, may require more targeted interventions. This finding is relevant to *RQ2*, as it highlights the differential effects of fairness interventions across protected attributes and the need for careful calibration of fairness constraints.

In summary, the results indicate a clear trade-off between fairness (as measured by micro and macro diversity gains) and utility, with the optimal λ values differing between race and country. This suggests that fairness policies should be tailored to the specific characteristics of each protected group to balance equity and quality effectively.

Table II presents the percentage of recommended papers from SIGCHI, DIS, and IUI across various fairness constraints. Regardless of the application of country-only, race-only, or multi-attribute fairness, SIGCHI papers maintain a dominant acceptance rate of approximately 92%, indicative of their elevated baseline acceptance rates. DIS and IUI contribute a modest but significant share of recommendations, suggesting that while SIGCHI retains prominence, the fairness constraints facilitate the inclusion of papers from smaller conferences without substantially affecting the overall distribution.

D. Ablation Study: Multi-Demographic Fairness

The objective of our ablation study was to evaluate the model's performance when optimizing fairness across multiple demographic attributes simultaneously, specifically with respect to both *country* and *race*. This ablation was conducted to address *RQ3*, which explores the impact of varying fairness weights for each attribute when multiple fairness attributes are considered together.

To ensure fairness, we removed these attributes from the input space, preventing the model from learning

TABLE IV. GAIN CALCULATIONS FOR COUNTRY AND RACE FEATURES WITH UTILITY GAIN.

λ	Weights	Country Feature		Race Feature		$UG_t(\%)$	Avg. $D_G(\%)$	Avg. F (%)
		Macro Gain (%)	Micro Gain (%)	Macro Gain (%)	Micro Gain (%)			
1	$W_r = 0.32, W_c = 0.68$	6.17	6.34	30.51	46.30	3.16	44.66	53.71
	$W_r = 1, W_c = 2$	6.73	9.15	-0.25	0.37	2.81	6.48	13.77
	$W_r = 2, W_c = 1$	7.43	11.43	12.91	16.11	3.16	25.63	40.36
2	$W_r = 0.32, W_c = 0.68$	**13.60**	**24.43**	30.51	42.22	**4.21**	55.38	68.47
	$W_r = 1, W_c = 2$	5.24	6.88	15.45	17.96	0.70	20.69	21.58
	$W_r = 2, W_c = 1$	8.36	12.86	39.49	54.26	1.75	26.31	21.58
2.5	$W_r = 0.32, W_c = 0.68$	8.63	17.33	36.58	50.37	2.46	56.46	66.31
	$W_r = 1, W_c = 2$	9.89	14.00	30.63	46.30	2.81	40.52	62.09
	$W_r = 2, W_c = 1$	9.60	17.11	42.53	56.48	1.40	59.25	69.98
3	$W_r = 0.32, W_c = 0.68$	7.15	11.42	39.49	53.89	1.40	55.98	63.45
	$W_r = 1, W_c = 2$	10.16	21.17	33.29	43.89	0.70	43.45	47.63
	$W_r = 2, W_c = 1$	9.60	18.35	42.53	55.37	2.81	61.90	47.63
5	$W_r = 0.32, W_c = 0.68$	10.80	19.38	**45.82**	**58.52**	0.70	**65.09**	**72.92**
	$W_r = 1, W_c = 2$	4.69	3.88	33.92	40.19	0.35	38.61	15.73
	$W_r = 2, W_c = 1$	7.43	11.90	39.49	52.96	5.26	52.26	15.73
10	$W_r = 0.32, W_c = 0.68$	9.60	18.34	42.53	55.37	1.40	62.92	70.89
	$W_r = 1, W_c = 2$	7.43	13.91	24.94	25.19	4.91	32.37	34.88
	$W_r = 2, W_c = 1$	7.43	11.72	35.44	47.41	-4.21	40.53	34.88

direct associations between them and the paper acceptance decisions. Instead, demographic parity loss was computed for each attribute during training, capturing deviations from fairness. The parity losses for both country and race were combined by assigning weights: W_c for country and W_r for race, with the initial weights set to $W_c = 0.68$ and $W_r = 0.32$, reflecting the distribution of protected groups.

To further explore the model's behavior and answer *RQ3*, we varied these weights, first increasing W_c while keeping W_r constant, and then increasing W_r while keeping W_c fixed. Additionally, we experimented with different values of the fairness regularization parameter λ, which controls the trade-off between fairness and utility. These experiments allowed us to observe how different weight configurations and fairness constraints influenced the model's ability to achieve demographic fairness while maintaining utility and the quality of selected papers.

The results of the ablation study, shown in Table IV, reveal that at $\lambda = 1$, assigning equal weights to both race and country ($W_r = 0.32, W_c = 0.68$) produced significant gains for race, with a Macro Gain of 30.51% and a Micro Gain of 46.3%, while country showed relatively smaller improvements (6.17% and 6.34%, respectively). However, when the weight for country was increased ($W_c = 2 \times 0.68$), diversity gains for race dropped sharply, with a negative Macro Gain (-0.25%), while country experienced slight improvements. Conversely, increasing the weight for race ($W_r = 2 \times 0.32$) resulted in improved diversity for both race and country, indicating that assigning more weight to race enhances diversity for both attributes to some degree.

At $\lambda = 2.5$, the model achieved the best balance between diversity and utility. Equal weights for race and country yielded Macro and Micro Gains of 36.58% and 50.37% for race, and 8.63% and 17.33% for country, with a low utility loss of 2.46%. This suggests that $\lambda = 2.5$ is optimal for balancing fairness and utility. As λ increases further, race diversity continues to improve (reaching 45.82% Macro Gain at $\lambda = 5$), but at the cost of decreasing utility. The different optimal λ values for race and country suggest that disparity ratios impact how fairness constraints should be weighted, with race requiring a higher λ due to its higher disparity ratio. This leads to greater race diversity gains at higher λ values, whereas country achieves optimal results at moderate λ values, such as 2.5.

These findings directly address *RQ3*, demonstrating that fairness weights must be carefully calibrated for each protected attribute. Assigning greater weight to race tends to improve diversity for both race and country, whereas increasing the weight for country may result in reduced fairness for race. The optimal balance between fairness and utility is achieved when fairness weights and λ values are adjusted based on the unique disparity ratios of each attribute.

VI. Conclusion and Future Work

This study introduces a fairness-oriented paper recommendation methodology that enhances demographic parity for race and country while maintaining academic quality. Our findings indicate that adjusting fairness requirements, including the regularization parameter λ and demographic weights, improves diversity while maintaining selection criteria.

Ablation experiments indicate that variations in race and country necessitate more stringent fairness requirements for optimal inclusion. Although beneficial, our technique lacks explicit causal modeling, which could enhance bias reduction. Investigating sophisticated designs such as Variational AutoEncoders (VAE) or graph-based models could enhance fairness and precision.

Incorporating institutional connections and combining causal fairness may improve bias mitigation. Confronting these obstacles will enhance fairness-oriented proposals, promoting a more inclusive peer review process.

ACKNOWLEDGMENT

This work was supported by the National Science Foundation (NSF) under Award number OIA-1946391, Data Analytics that are Robust and Trusted (DART).

REFERENCES

[1] A. Tomkins, M. Zhang, and W. Heavlin, "Reviewer bias in single- versus double-blind peer review," *Proceedings of the National Academy of Sciences of the United States of America*, vol. 114, pp. 12 708–12 713, 2017. DOI: 10 . 1073 / pnas . 1707323114.

[2] E. Shmidt and B. Jacobson, "Double-blind reviews: A step toward eliminating unconscious bias," *Clinical and Translational Gastroenterology*, vol. 13, no. 1, e00443, 2022. DOI: 10.14309/ctg.0000000000000443.

[3] V. P. Giannakakos, T. S. Karanfilian, A. D. Dimopoulos, and A. Barmettler, "Impact of author characteristics on outcomes of single- versus double-blind peer review: A systematic review of comparative studies in scientific abstracts and publications," *Scientometrics*, vol. 130, pp. 399–421, 2025. DOI: 10.1007/s11192-024-05213-x.

[4] C. Mebane, "Double-blind peer review is detrimental to scientific integrity," *Environmental Toxicology and Chemistry*, vol. 44, pp. 318–323, 2025. DOI: 10.1093/etojnl/vgae046.

[5] L. Bauersfeld, A. Romero, M. Muglikar, and D. Scaramuzza, "Cracking double-blind review: Authorship attribution with deep learning," *PLoS ONE*, vol. 18, no. 6, e0287611, Jun. 2023. DOI: 10.1371/journal.pone.0287611.

[6] N. B. Shah, "The role of author identities in peer review," *PLOS ONE*, vol. 18, no. 6, e0286206, Jun. 2023. DOI: 10.1371/journal.pone.0286206.

[7] J. Huber *et al.*, "Nobel and novice: Author prominence affects peer review," *Proceedings of the National Academy of Sciences of the United States of America*, vol. 119, no. 41, e2205779119, 2022. DOI: 10.1073/pnas.2205779119.

[8] E. Frachtenberg and K. McConville, "Metrics and methods in the evaluation of prestige bias in peer review: A case study in computer systems conferences," *PLoS ONE*, vol. 17, e0264131, 2022. DOI: 10.1371/journal.pone.0264131.

[9] C. J. Lee, C. R. Sugimoto, G. Zhang, and B. Cronin, "Bias in peer review," *Journal of the American Society for Information Science and Technology*, vol. 64, no. 1, pp. 2–17, 2013. DOI: 10.1002/asi.22784.

[10] C. L. Goues *et al.*, "Effectiveness of anonymization in double-blind review," *Communications of the ACM*, vol. 61, pp. 30–33, 2017. DOI: 10.1145/3208157.

[11] J. Bobadilla, R. Lara-Cabrera, Á. González-Prieto, and F. Ortega, "DeepFair: Deep learning for improving fairness in recommender systems," *Information Processing & Management*, vol. 58, no. 3, p. 102 547, May 2021. DOI: 10.1016/j.ipm.2021.102547.

[12] Y. Peng, X. Qian, and W. Song, "A re-ranking approach for two-sided fairness on recommendation systems," in *Proceedings of the 2023 4th International Conference on Computing, Networks and Internet of Things*, May 2023, pp. 312–316. DOI: 10.1145/3603781.3603836.

[13] K. Morik *et al.*, "Controlling fairness and bias in dynamic learning-to-rank," in *Proceedings of the 29th ACM International Conference on Information & Knowledge Management (CIKM)*, 2020, pp. 267–276. DOI: 10.1145/3340531.3412875.

[14] A. Beutel, J. Chen, Z. Zhao, and E. H. Chi, *Data decisions and theoretical implications when adversarially learning fair representations*, FAT/ML 2017 Workshop, 2017.

[15] S. Yao and B. Huang, "Beyond parity: Fairness objectives for collaborative filtering," in *Advances in Neural Information Processing Systems (NeurIPS)*, Focuses on equality of opportunity and calibration in CF., vol. 30, 2017.

[16] J. A. Bol, A. Sheffel, N. Zia, and A. Meghani, "How to address the geographical bias in academic publishing," *BMJ Glob Health*, vol. 8, no. 12, e013111, Dec. 2023. DOI: 10.1136/bmjgh-2023-013111.

[17] C. J. Lee, C. R. Sugimoto, G. Zhang, and B. Cronin, "Bias in peer review," *J. Assoc. Inf. Sci. Technol.*, vol. 64, pp. 2–17, 2013. DOI: 10.1002/ASI.22784.

[18] W. M. Williams and S. J. Ceci, "National hiring experiments reveal 2:1 faculty preference for women on STEM tenure track," eng, *Proceedings of the National Academy of Sciences of the United States of America*, vol. 112, no. 17, pp. 5360–5365, Apr. 2015, ISSN: 1091-6490. DOI: 10.1073/pnas.1418878112.

[19] R. Burke, "Multisided fairness for recommendation," in *Proceedings of the ACM RecSys '17 Workshop on Responsible Recommendation*, Como, Italy: ACM, Aug. 2017, pp. 1–4. DOI: 10.1145/3109859.3109962.

[20] R. Alsaffar and S. Gauch, "Multidimensional demographic profiles for fair paper recommendation," in *Proceedings of the 13th International Joint Conference on Knowledge Discovery, Knowledge Engineering and Knowledge Management (IC3K 2021)*, Online: SCITEPRESS - Science and Technology Publications, Oct. 2021, pp. 199–208, ISBN: 978-989-758-533-3. DOI: 10.5220/0010655800003064.

[21] Z. Fu *et al.*, "Fairness-aware explainable recommendation over knowledge graphs," in *Proceedings of the 43rd International ACM SIGIR Conference on Research and Development in Information Retrieval*, Jul. 2020, pp. 69–78. DOI: 10.1145/3397271.3401051.

[22] R. Islam, K. N. Keya, Z. Zeng, S. Pan, and J. Foulds, "Neural Fair Collaborative Filtering," in *Proceedings of the 15th ACM Conference on Recommender Systems (RecSys '21)*, Proposes a multi-task learning approach for fairness in neural collaborative filtering., Amsterdam, Netherlands: ACM, Sep. 2021, pp. 148–159. DOI: 10.1145/3460231.3474603.

[23] H. Wu, C. Ma, B. Mitra, F. Diaz, and X. Liu, "A multi-objective optimization framework for multi-stakeholder fairness-aware recommendation," *ACM Transactions on Information Systems (TOIS)*, vol. 41, no. 2, 47:1–47:29, 2022. DOI: 10 . 1145 / 3564285.

[24] Y. Wang, W. Ma, M. Zhang, Y. Liu, and S. Ma, "A survey on the fairness of recommender systems," *ACM Transactions on Information Systems (TOIS)*, vol. 41, no. 3, 52:1–52:43, 2023. DOI: 10.1145/3547333.

[25] B. Bulut, B. Kaya, R. Alhajj, and M. Kaya, "A paper recommendation system based on user's research interests," in *2018 IEEE/ACM International Conference on Advances in Social Networks Analysis and Mining (ASONAM)*, 2018, pp. 911–915. DOI: 10.1109/ASONAM.2018.8508313.

ColBERT-Based User Profiles for Personalized Information Retrieval

Aleena Ahmad*, Gibson Nkhata†, Abdul Rafay Bajwa‡, Hannah Marsico†, Bryan Le†, Susan Gauch†

†Department of Electrical Engineering and Computer Science,
University of Arkansas, Fayetteville, USA
Email: {gnkhata, hmarsico, bryanle, sgauch}@uark.edu

‡Syed Babar Ali School of Science and Engineering,
Lahore University of Management Sciences, Lahore,
Pakistan
Email: 25100194@lums.edu.pk

*School of Electrical Engineering and Computer Science,
National University of Sciences and Technology, Islamabad, Pakistan
Email: alahmad.bscs21seecs@seecs.edu.pk

Abstract—**Personalized Information Retrieval (PIR) improves search relevance by tailoring results to user interests using query history and browsing patterns. Traditional approaches to personalization range from feature engineering to the use of ontologies. Recently, there has been an increase in the exploration of deep learning models for this purpose. These models, such as Contextual Late Interaction over Bidirectional Encoder Representations from Transformers (ColBERT), provide token-level contextual embeddings that can be leveraged to generate semantic user profiles. State-of-the-art approaches use ColBERT to select candidate terms for personalized query expansion from user profiles. This approach poses challenges in accurately choosing user's descriptive keywords, risking the omission of crucial user preferences and repetitive selection of user terms. This study proposes a novel PIR approach that fully encodes user profiles using contextual embeddings and reranks Best Matching 25 (BM25) retrieved documents. Additionally, a frequency-recency weighting mechanism is tested which adjusts query influence based on temporal proximity and repetition frequency. Experimental results on two publicly available datasets demonstrate that our method improves retrieval performance, providing more accurate and context-aware search results.**

Keywords-Personalized information retrieval; user profile generation; ColBERT; reranking algorithms.

I. INTRODUCTION

With the exponential growth and complexity of information on the Web, it has been a daunting task for users to find relevant and interesting information [1]. Hence, Personalized Information Retrieval (PIR) was introduced to tailor search results according to a user's preferences and context, leveraging user-specific data such as query history, clicked documents, and browsing patterns. Unlike traditional retrieval systems that deliver uniform results, PIR systems dynamically adapt to user behavior, significantly enhancing relevance and search efficiency [2]–[4]. This evolution has been driven by advances in user profile modeling, semantic ontologies, and machine learning techniques.

The advent of deep learning and pre-trained language models, such as Bidirectional Encoder Representations from Transformers (BERT) [5], has revolutionized PIR. Models, such as Contextual Late Interaction over BERT (ColBERT) [6], which builds on top of BERT and combines token-level contextual embeddings with efficient retrieval mechanisms, have demonstrated superior performance. ColBERT enhances traditional retrieval methods like Best Matching 25 (BM25) [7] by reranking search results using token-level BERT embeddings. This hybrid approach has proven effective, as evidenced by its application in reranking documents retrieved by BM25 through query expansion [8][9]. On the same note, [9] employs a clustering-based procedure and uses ColBERT embeddings to identify the terms most representative of the user interests to be used for query expansion. Existing methods primarily use contextual word embeddings to select limited terms from user profiles for query expansion [9]–[12], as a result, risking the omission of crucial user preferences and repetitive selection of user's descriptive terms.

This work aims to overcome these limitations by integrating entire user profiles in the personalization approach. The major contributions of this work are outlined as follows:

1) **Full User Profile Representation:** Unlike previous methods which rely on term extraction, this work explores the impact of representing complete user profiles using contextual token-level embeddings, preserving all aspects of user preferences.
2) **Frequency-Recency Weighting Mechanism:** A novel weighting strategy is explored that combines the effect of query recency and frequency. An exponential decay function models temporal influence, while a logarithmic function balances frequent queries.
3) **Personalized Reranking with ColBERT:** ColBERT embeddings are leveraged as a second-stage algorithm to rerank candidate documents retrieved by BM25, ensuring more effective and context-aware personalization compared to term-based query expansion techniques.

The remainder of this paper is organized as follows. Section II reviews related work in PIR. Section III presents our proposed methodology, including user profile construction and our personalization model. Section IV details the experimental setup, datasets, and evaluation metrics. Finally, Section V concludes the paper, highlighting key findings and discussing directions for future work.

II. Related work

This section presents related work on PIR. Early work on PIR employed matching user profile keywords, extracted from previously visited documents, with document vectors by adapting the vector space model [2][13][14]. For example, [14] represents both user profiles and documents as vectors within the same term space, often derived from tags or keywords. The user profile vector encapsulates the user's interests based on previously interacted tags, while the document vector represents the content's tag distribution. This is an easy approach, but it still has shortfalls, e.g., the same user profile keyword can have multiple meanings, like bank as a financial institution vs. bank of a river, and dimensionality inconsistency between keywords and document vectors, leading to irrelevant retrieved results.

To address ambiguity issues, other researchers used ontologies to model user profiles [3][4]. For example, [3] adapts the navigation of information based on a user profile structured as a weighted concept hierarchy. Specifically, every web page visited by a user is classified into this concept hierarchy, and the resulting ontologies are then used for either reranking search results or filtering relevant documents. This approach combated the polysemy problem associated with keywords, still, it lacks context awareness, as deep semantic relationships among words in the documents are not encoded by the ontological user profiles.

Because of their ability to capture words in context, state-of-the-art approaches to PIR use pre-trained word embeddings to model documents and user profiles [6][8][15][16]. These techniques merely leverage contextual word embeddings for query expansion.

While recent work has employed pre-trained word embeddings for PIR, it has not exploited them to fully represent user profile information. As described in the aforementioned works, retrospectively, the common practice in incorporating embeddings is to use them to select terms from the user profile to expand the user query. While this provides personalization, some crucial user information may be overlooked by the selection process, and sometimes, the same terms might habitually be selected from the user profile as candidates for query expansion. Our work, on the other hand, deviates from literature by incorporating the entire user profile into the retrieval process, instead of using it to extract expansion terms. It generates an embedding-based representation of the entire profile, which is used directly to rerank results returned by BM25.

III. Methodology

This section describes the methodology employed to develop and evaluate the proposed approach. The first step was selecting and preprocessing datasets suitable for testing personalization. Next, user profiles were generated using user histories and provided as input for the personalization model. Finally, the results are reranked by the personalization model. Each of these steps is detailed in the following subsections.

A. Dataset and Preprocessing

Experiments on personalization require user-specific data, such as previously issued queries, clicked documents, etc. [3] Two publicly available datasets suitable for this purpose were used.

*1) **AOL4PS** :* This is a dataset generated from the American Online (AOL) query logs. The authors [17] processed the original query logs to construct a dataset suitable for personalization. Each query record has an associated user id, timestamp, session information, the Uniform Resource Locators (URLs) of the top ten retrieved documents, and the index position of the clicked document. The original dataset statistics are presented in Table I.

TABLE I. AOL4PS STATISTICS

Metric	Value
Total number of records	1,339,101
Number of users	12,907
Average number of records per user	103.75
Unique records per user (mean)	47.23

The dataset only included URLs for documents - not textual content - which was required for building user profiles and computing similarity. Hence, the first step was to download the textual content of each URL by scraping the web. Given the dataset's age, many of the URLs in the dataset were no longer available. To recover historical content, the Wayback Machine [18] was used where possible. Each URL was retained only if it was accessible and had sufficient content to be used meaningfully for indexing and similarity computation. This filtering found only **158,235** URLs from the original **951,941** to be valid. Based on these available URLs, we applied the following record-level filtering:

- Records were removed if the **clicked URL** was not available.
- Records were removed if none of the **10 retrieved documents** were available.

The statistics of the filtered data are presented in Table II. The number of records overall and per-user was considerably reduced post-filtering. Further filtering was done before a sample of test users could be extracted, the details of which are presented in Section IV.

TABLE II. DATASET STATISTICS AFTER INITIAL FILTERING

Metric	Value
Total number of records	276,459
Number of users	12,493
Average number of records per user	22.13
Unique records per user (mean)	11.04

*2) **Personalized Results Reranking Benchmark (PRRB)**:* This is a multi-domain dataset, proposed by [9], used for personalized search evaluation. It consists of datasets divided into four domains: Computer Science, Physics, Psychology, and Political Science. It has a total of 1.9 million queries divided across these four domains. The PERSON methodology [19] was used for the construction of the dataset, using published papers to develop triplets of users, queries, and documents. In particular, a paper's title is considered as a query, one of the authors is considered as the user, and the referenced papers are considered as relevant documents. Detailed statistics of the datasets are presented in Table III.

B. Profile Generation

To create representative profiles, we gathered the available data from each user's history. Based on the approaches previously followed [17], we incorporated relevant documents and previously issued queries. The queries issued by users are a direct statement of interest; hence they were included. Similarly, the title and content of the clicked document were included, as they were the ones that the user considered relevant for a particular query.

For a given user u, their profile P_u is constructed by concatenating their past issued queries and clicked documents:

The user profile P_u is represented as:

$$P_u = (Q_u, D_u)$$

where:

- Q_u is the set of past queries issued by the user:

$$Q_u = \{q_1, q_2, \dots, q_N\}$$

- D_u represents the set of past clicked documents (titles and content):

$$D_u = \{d_1, d_2, \dots, d_M\}$$

where: - N is the number of past queries. - M is the number of past clicked documents.

Each document d_i consists of a title t_i and content c_i:

$$d_i = [t_i, c_i]$$

Thus, the final profile representation can be expressed as:

$$P_u = \left(\sum_{i=1}^{N} q_i, \sum_{j=1}^{M} (t_j, c_j) \right)$$

For each dataset, the profile generation process is detailed below:

*1) **AOL4PS**:* As stated in Section III-B above, the associated information with each user in this dataset includes the text of previously issued queries and the corresponding clicked documents for each query.

*2) **PRRB**:* For this dataset, each user's issued queries were titles of the papers authored by the user. The documents in a user's profile were other papers authored by this user. For consistency with AOL4PS, the papers' titles and contents are analogous to user's past queries and clicked-on retrieved documents, respectively.

C. Personalization Model

The final content of a user's profile is represented as contextual word embeddings. The embedding model used for this purpose is ColBERT v2 [6].

The personalization approach tested in this work consists of the following steps:

1) Prior to testing, all documents originally retrieved for each test query are obtained, represented as embeddings, and indexed with ColBERT. This happens in an offline stage.
2) When testing, two arguments are passed to ColBERT's searcher:
   - The 'query' against which the documents will be ranked. In our case, the user profile serves as the query.
   - The list of document IDs that were originally retrieved for the given query. This ensures that the similarity calculation and reranking is done only for the associated documents of a query, instead of the entire index.
3) In cases where the user profile exceeds ColBERT's 32-token limit, it is split into 32-token chunks. Each chunk then separately reranks the associated documents.
4) The results of each chunk are aggregated using maximum pooling, allowing a document to have a high score if it matches any chunk of the user's profile. These aggregated results then become the final reranked document list against a query.

In addition to this basic approach, the Frequency-Recency approach is tested which differs in how the profile is used to rerank the results.

*1) **Frequency-Recency Approach**:* This approach incorporates frequency and recency information of a query into the reranking process. Each query in the dataset had an associated timestamp, which is used to calculate the time difference between it and the currently tested query. In addition, repetitions of queries are taken into consideration.To adjust the influence of past queries based on their time of occurrence and repetition, we define the following weighting functions:

Recency-Based Weighting: We hypothesize that user queries issued in the past may become less relevant over time. To model this, we apply an *exponential decay function*, which reduces the weight of older queries:

$$w_{\text{recency},i} = e^{-\alpha \cdot \Delta t_i} \quad (1)$$

where:

- $w_{\text{recency},i}$ is the recency weight assigned to the historical query i.
- Δt_i is the time difference (in days) between the test query and the past query.
- α is a decay parameter that controls how quickly the influence of older queries diminishes.

A higher value of α causes past queries to decay faster, reducing their contribution to reranking.

Frequency-Based Weighting: Users often repeat queries when searching for specific information. Queries that appear frequently in a user's history likely indicate stronger preferences.

TABLE III. STATISTICS OF THE DATASETS

	PRRB			
	Computer Science	Physics	Political Science	Psychology
# documents	4 809 684	4 926 753	4 814 084	4 215 384
# users	5 260 279	5 835 016	6 347 092	4 825 578
# train queries	552 798	728 171	162 597	544 882
# validation queries	5 583	7 355	1 642	5 503
# test queries	6 497	6 366	5 715	12 625
# sessions	-	-	-	-
# clicked documents	-	-	-	-

To account for this, we apply a logarithmic transformation to query frequency:

$$w_{\text{frequency},i} = \log(1 + \beta \cdot f_i) \quad (2)$$

where:

- $w_{\text{frequency},i}$ is the frequency weight for query i.
- f_i is the number of times query i has been issued by the user.
- β is a scaling factor that controls the influence of frequency on the final weight.

Using a logarithm ensures that the effect of very high frequencies is moderated, preventing overly frequent queries from dominating the reranking.

Final Weighting Function: To combine both recency and frequency effects, the final query-document pair weight is computed as:

$$w_i = w_{\text{recency},i} \cdot w_{\text{frequency},i} = e^{-\alpha \cdot \Delta t_i} \cdot \log(1 + \beta \cdot f_i) \quad (3)$$

where:

- w_i is the overall weight assigned to the query-document pair.
- The recency term $e^{-\alpha \cdot \Delta t_i}$ ensures that older queries have less influence.
- The frequency term $\log(1 + \beta \cdot f_i)$ ensures frequently issued queries have greater weight.

Prior research has shown the effectiveness of exponential decay in modeling recency [20] and log-based frequency weighting in ranking models [21]. The values of α and β are tuned experimentally to optimize performance. Figure 1 illustrates the entire model framework.

IV. EXPERIMENTS

This section delves into the experimental details of this work.

A. Experimental Setup

To use ColBERT, we utilized the Python RAGatouille [22] library. This is a framework for easier access and setup of ColBERT, particularly when using Google Colab, where all our experiments were conducted. It provides all functionalities that can be used with barebone ColBERT.

*1) **AOL4PS**:* In addition to the process described in Section III-B, further filtering was performed to ensure constant profile size across a set of users. To do so, users were classified into buckets based on the number of query records available for profile creation. The distribution of the number of query records per users was observed, and the following buckets were chosen **10-15, 16-25, 26-35, 36-45, 46-above records.** Each bucket had an associated profile length, shown in Table IV. This excluded users with fewer than 10 valid records, which formed a major proportion of the filtered dataset. The records of the remaining users were divided into train and test sets. For this, the records were first sorted by time. The initial n records were chosen for the train set (to build user profiles), where n was equal to the profile length of the bucket.

TABLE IV. USER BUCKETS AND ASSOCIATED PROFILE LENGTHS

Bucket	Tested Profile Length
10-15	5
16-25	10
26-35	20
36-45	30
46 and above	40

For the test set, the remaining records for each user after extracting train set were chosen. From these, only the records where at least 5 of the URLs originally retrieved against the query were available were kept. This ensured our ranking of the clicked document was standardized.

In both sets, to ensure that all records did not consist of repeated queries, the number of repeated queries was limited to 1/3rd of the length of the records in the set.

As a result, 349 users remained that satisfied the aforementioned filtering and bucketing strategy. These were all useed for testing. and satisfied the filtering criteria and bucketing strategy described above. The distribution of these 349 users across each bucket, and other statistics, are shown in Table V.

Each user bucket was tested not only with its assigned profile length but also with all smaller profile lengths from lower buckets, enabling analysis of how profile size impacts personalization performance.

*2) **PRRB**:* For this dataset, a random sample of 1000 queries was selected from each domain and tested with the baseline and

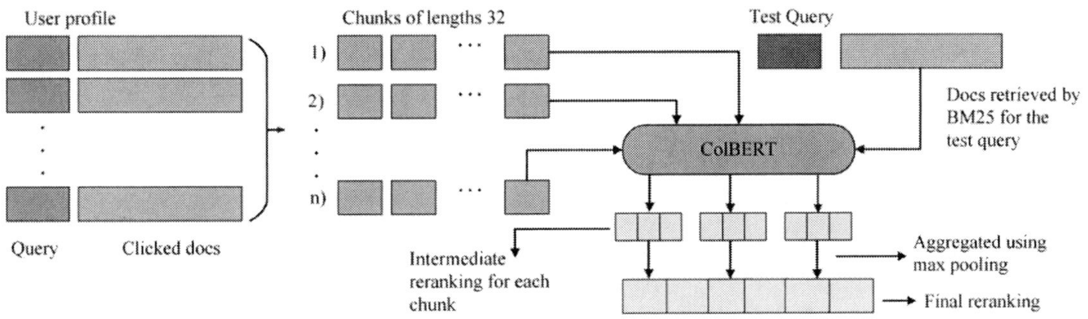

Figure 1: The model framework.

TABLE V. USER BUCKET STATISTICS

Bucket	# Users	# Train Records	# Test Records
10-15	56	280	295
16-25	157	1570	858
26-35	43	860	229
36-45	18	540	94
46 and above	75	3000	569

personalization model. Statistics for this sample are presented in Table VI.

TABLE VI. PRRB STATISTICS FOR SAMPLE 1000.

Domain	# Users	# User Docs	# Docs/User (Avg)
Computer Science	881	78 516	104
Physics	803	61 394	104
Psychology	937	70 399	84
Political Science	837	38038	52

B. Evaluation Metrics

To evaluate the performance of the considered models, the following metrics are employed: (1) Mean Average Precision (MAP), (2) Mean Reciprocal Rank (MRR), as primary evaluation metrics.

*1) **MAP**:* The average precision of the relevant retrieved documents averaged across a set of queries.

*2) **MRR**:* The average of the reciprocal ranks of the first relevant result for a set of queries.

C. Baselines

This section introduces the baselines employed in the comparative evaluation. First, our model is compared with BM25, to assess whether our approach can effectively rerank retrieved documents. Then we consider personalized query expansion approaches based on word embeddings, to verify if our proposed approach is improving over the state-of-the-art techniques. Similar to our work, personalized query expansion techniques are second-stage retrieval algorithms, where BM25 is a first-stage retriever.

1) **BM25** [7]: A ranking function that scores documents based on their relevance to a given query. It uses Term Frequency (tf), Inverse Document Frequency (idf), and document length normalization.
2) **ColBERT-PRF** [10]: A query expansion method based on ColBERT with reliance on Pseudo-Relevance Feedback (PRF) [23]. Given a query, it first ranks the documents using ColBERT, then clusters the term embeddings of a certain number of feedback documents with k-means clustering algorithm and selects the tokens corresponding to the cluster centroids with higher idf scores for query expansion.
3) **Query Expansion for Email Search (QEES)** [11]: A query expansion approach that begins by calculating the cosine similarity between each user-related term embedding and every query term embedding. These similarity scores are then transformed into a probability distribution using softmax normalization. Finally, the method aggregates the log probabilities for each user-related term embedding and selects the highest-scoring terms to expand the query.
4) **Query Expansion with Enriched User Profiles (QEEUP)** [12]: A query expansion technique that computes the cosine similarities among the user-related term embeddings and the sum of the query term embeddings and selects the top-scored ones for expanding the query.
5) **Personalized Query Expansion with Contextual Word Embeddings (PQEWC)** [15]: A query expansion technique that builds on ColBERT and devises HDBSCAN [24], a hierarchical density-based clustering method, to identify the terms that better represent the user interests.

Since these baselines' setups are inconsistent with AOL4S, they are evaluated on PRRB only, while AOL4S is used for comparing various derivations of our model.

D. Results

Table VII shows PRRB results using MAP@100 and MRR@10, reflecting the top 100 and 10 reranked results, respectively. Table VIII presents AOL4PS results using MRR@10 and MAP@1. These metrics correspond to previous work in PIR with these datasets, such as [15], [25]. Best scores per domain or bucket are shown in bold. Additional testing of the Personalization Approach with different profile lengths for

TABLE VII. EXPERIMENTAL RESULTS ON PRRB.

Model	Computer Science		Physics		Psychology		Political Science	
	MAP@100	MRR@10	MAP@100	MRR@10	MAP@100	MRR@10	MAP@100	MRR@10
BM25	0.1511	0.4826	0.1295	0.5551	0.2122	0.6297	0.1713	0.5430
ColBERT-PRF	0.1856	0.5682	0.1877	0.6150	0.2192	0.6253	0.1642	0.5351
QEES	0.1813	0.5632	0.1783	0.6118	0.2142	0.6285	0.1598	0.5305
QEEUP	0.1818	0.5686	0.1805	0.6256	0.2137	0.6276	0.1549	0.5285
PQEWC	0.1903	0.5766	0.1917	0.6381	0.2230	0.6421	0.1724	0.5510
Ours	**0.2026**	**0.5871**	**0.1919**	**0.6495**	**0.2278**	**0.6493**	**0.1840**	**0.5694**

TABLE VIII. EXPERIMENTAL RESULTS ON AOL4PS.

Buckets	BM25		ColBERT Non Personalized		Personalization Approach		Recency-Frequency	
	MRR@10	MAP@1	MRR@10	MAP@1	MRR@10	MAP@1	MRR@10	MAP@1
10-15	0.3311	0.1559	0.3671	0.1322	**0.5723**	0.2780	0.5285	**0.2848**
16-25	0.3249	0.1480	0.3789	0.1317	**0.5822**	**0.2984**	0.5304	0.2879
26-35	0.3188	0.1222	0.3906	0.1354	**0.5921**	**0.3188**	0.5186	0.2751
36-45	0.4160	0.2553	0.3425	0.0957	**0.6447**	**0.3404**	0.5111	0.2660
46-above	0.3452	0.1706	0.3684	0.1255	**0.6463**	**0.3667**	0.5102	0.2647

TABLE IX. TESTING WITH DIFFERENT PROFILE LENGTHS

Buckets	5		10		20		30		40	
	MRR@10	MAP@1	MRR@10	MAP@1	MRR@10	MAP@1	MRR@10	MAP@1	MRR@10	MAP@1
10-15	**0.5723**	**0.2780**	-	-	-	-	-	-	-	-
16-25	0.4433	0.0991	**0.5822**	**0.2984**	-	-	-	-	-	-
26-35	0.4203	0.1004	0.4438	0.1223	**0.5921**	**0.3188**	-	-	-	-
36-45	0.4247	0.1064	0.4404	0.1383	0.4679	0.1596	**0.6447**	**0.3404**	-	-
46-above	0.4718	0.1176	0.4735	0.1255	0.4877	0.1353	0.4918	0.1294	**0.6463**	**0.3667**

each bucket are shown in Table IX, allowing for an analysis on how profile length effects personalization effectiveness.

E. Discussion

It can be observed that the proposed personalization approach consistently outperforms the baselines in each test setup. In experiments with the PRRB dataset, the personalization approach outperforms BM25 and other baseline query-expansion methods. Most notably, the greatest improvement in MRR@10 is observed in Computer Science and Physics. The query expansion techniques in Table VII employ pre-trained word embeddings in selecting terms to expand the query, thus outperforming the baseline. Still, they struggle against our method because we use contextual word embeddings to encode the entire user profile, thereby encoding subtle nuances and attributes that help in reranking relevant documents for PIR.

For the AOL4PS dataset, the use of contextual embeddings, with or without personalization, consistently outperforms the BM25 baseline across all buckets and profile sizes. A discrepancy is observed in the 36-45 bucket, where the *ColBERT Non Personalized* approach's results are lower than the BM25 results. This may be due to data limitations or statistical variance. However, the overall trend indicates that personalization significantly enhances ranking effectiveness, particularly as user profile data increases. This is supported by the fact that greater bucket sizes (which corresponds to the amount of data used for profile generation) correspond to higher MRR values.

Furthermore, the results in Table IX show that, for each set of users, the MRR and MAP values generally increase as the profile size increases. The best performance is seen when the greatest number of records are incorporated in the profile.

The recency-frequency weighting approach, while not surpassing our base personalization model, does offer improvements against the BM25 and ColBERT Non-Personalized approaches. An interesting observation is that it performs better with smaller user profiles. This could imply that, with sufficient user history, the need to integrate recency and frequency diminishes and the information needed for personalization can be obtained from the textual content of the profile itself.

Response Time Analysis:
The indexing of documents and the creation of user profiles occur offline, before testing. At runtime, similarity calculations are performed between the user profile chunks with each document and the results are aggregated. Hence, the response time for each query depends on the length of the user profile (number of documents incorporated). The average response times for each profile length when tested with the proposed Personalization approach are summarized in Table X. These times are observed from experimentation done with Google Colab's A100 GPU.

Memory Analysis:

TABLE X. PROFILE LENGTHS AND AVERAGE RESPONSE TIME PER QUERY

Profile Length	Average Response Time (s)
5	3.69
10	7.04
20	14.37
30	22.11
40	29.85

The personalized approach stores the top-k candidate documents and the user profile in memory to compute similarity scores. Memory usage thus depends on the number of documents per profile and the candidate set size.

For AOL4PS, with k = 10 and an average document size of 9 KB, candidate documents require 90 KB. Including the profile, total memory ranges from 135 KB (5-document profile) to 450 KB (40-document profile).

For PRRB, k = 100 and average document size 1 KB, yielding 100 KB for candidates. Including the profile, total memory ranges from 105 KB to 140 KB for 5–40 document profiles.

V. Conclusion and Future Work

This work presents a novel PIR approach that encodes entire user profiles using contextual word embeddings and re-ranks BM25 retrieved documents. Additionally, it tests a frequency-recency weighting mechanism to study the impact of temporal proximity and repetition on personalization performance. Through experimentation on two publicly available datasets, the effectiveness of our approach is confirmed. For the PRRB dataset, our proposed personalization model consistently outperforms BM25 ranking and query-expansion baselines. For the AOL4PS dataset, personalization improves ranking across all user profile sizes, with larger profiles showing better results. The recency-frequency approach offers improvements relative to the baseline, however it benefits users with limited search history more. Overall, this work reinforces the idea that utilizing complete user profiles for PIR is an effective approach. It also highlights the potential of deep learning-based methods to develop rich representations.

Further work can build on the limitations of our study. Our testing with AOL4PS involved a small user sample due to limited valid URLs. Expanding URL scrapping to different geographic locations could increase access to URLs, allowing a greater number of valid records and users for testing. Future work can also study profiling techniques which integrate session information and provide efficient scaling for real-time personalization.

Acknowledgment

This work was supported by the National Science Foundation under Award number OIA-1946391, Data Analytics that are Robust and Trusted (DART).

References

[1] S. Gauch, "Conceptual recommender system for citeseerx", 2009.

[2] N. J. Belkin and W. B. Croft, "Retrieval techniques", *Annual Review of Information Science and Technology (ARIST)*, vol. 28, pp. 109–145, 1993.

[3] S. Gauch, J. Chaffee, and A. Pretschner, "Ontology-based personalized search and browsing", *Web Intelligence and Agent Systems: An international Journal*, vol. 1, no. 3-4, pp. 219–234, 2003.

[4] A. Sieg, B. Mobasher, and R. Burke, "Web search personalization with ontological user profiles", in *Proceedings of the sixteenth ACM conference on Conference on information and knowledge management*, 2007, pp. 525–534.

[5] J. Devlin, "Bert: Pre-training of deep bidirectional transformers for language understanding", *arXiv preprint arXiv:1810.04805*, 2018.

[6] O. Khattab and M. Zaharia, "Colbert: Efficient and effective passage search via contextualized late interaction over bert", in *Proceedings of the 43rd International ACM SIGIR conference on research and development in Information Retrieval*, 2020, pp. 39–48.

[7] S. E. Robertson, S. Walker, S. Jones, M. M. Hancock-Beaulieu, and M. Gatford, "Okapi at trec-3: At the interface between probabilistic and vector space models", in *Proceedings of the Third Text REtrieval Conference (TREC-3)*, National Institute of Standards and Technology (NIST), 1994, pp. 109–126.

[8] A. Salemi, S. Kallumadi, and H. Zamani, "Optimization methods for personalizing large language models through retrieval augmentation", *arXiv preprint arXiv:2404.05970*, 2024.

[9] E. Bassani, P. Kasela, A. Raganato, and G. Pasi, "A multi-domain benchmark for personalized search evaluation", in *Proceedings of the 31st ACM International Conference on Information & Knowledge Management*, 2022, pp. 3822–3827.

[10] X. Wang, C. Macdonald, N. Tonellotto, and I. Ounis, "Pseudo-relevance feedback for multiple representation dense retrieval", in *Proceedings of the 2021 ACM SIGIR International Conference on Theory of Information Retrieval*, 2021, pp. 297–306.

[11] S. Kuzi, D. Carmel, A. Libov, and A. Raviv, "Query expansion for email search", in *Proceedings of the 40th International ACM SIGIR Conference on Research and Development in Information Retrieval*, 2017, pp. 849–852.

[12] D. Zhou, X. Wu, W. Zhao, S. Lawless, and J. Liu, "Query expansion with enriched user profiles for personalized search utilizing folksonomy data", *IEEE Transactions on Knowledge and Data Engineering*, vol. 29, no. 7, pp. 1536–1548, 2017.

[13] G. Salton, A. Wong, and C. Yang, "A vector space model for automatic indexing", *Communications of the ACM*, vol. 18, no. 11, pp. 613–620, 1975.

[14] Z. Xu, J. Zhang, J. Li, and J. Li, "Personalized information retrieval through user profile based document filtering", in *Proceedings of the 2008 IEEE International Conference on Information and Automation*, IEEE, 2008, pp. 1861–1865.

[15] E. Bassani, N. Tonellotto, and G. Pasi, "Personalized query expansion with contextual word embeddings", *ACM Transactions on Information Systems*, vol. 42, no. 2, pp. 1–35, 2023.

[16] C. Richardson *et al.*, "Integrating summarization and retrieval for enhanced personalization via large language models", *arXiv preprint arXiv:2310.20081*, 2023.

[17] Q. Guo, W. Chen, and H. Wan, "Aol4ps: A large-scale data set for personalized search", *Data Intelligence*, vol. 3, no. 4, pp. 548–567, Oct. 2021, ISSN: 2641-435X. DOI: 10.1162/dint_a_00104. eprint: https://direct.mit.edu/dint/article-pdf/3/4/548/1968580/dint_a_00104.pdf.

[18] I. Archive, *Wayback machine*, Accessed April 5, 2025.

[19] S. A. Tabrizi, A. Shakery, H. Zamani, and M. A. Tavallaei, "Person: Personalized information retrieval evaluation based on citation networks", *Information Processing & Management*, vol. 54, no. 4, pp. 630–656, 2018.

[20] P. Ardagelou and A. Arampatzis, "A half-life decaying model for recommender systems with matrix factorization", in *TDDL/MDQual/Futurity@ TPDL*, 2017.

[21] D. Vianna and A. Marian, "A frequency-based learning-to-rank approach for personal digital traces", *arXiv preprint arXiv:2012.13114*, 2020.

[22] B. Clavié, *Ragatouille*, version 0.0.9, Available at: https://github.com/AnswerDotAI/RAGatouille, 2023.

[23] J. J. Rocchio Jr, "Relevance feedback in information retrieval", *The SMART retrieval system: experiments in automatic document processing*, 1971.

[24] L. McInnes, J. Healy, and S. Astels, "Hdbscan: Hierarchical density based clustering.", *J. Open Source Softw.*, vol. 2, no. 11, p. 205, 2017.

[25] J. Yao, Z. Dou, and J.-R. Wen, "Employing personal word embeddings for personalized search", in *Proceedings of the 43rd international ACM SIGIR conference on research and development in information retrieval*, 2020, pp. 1359–1368.

Identification and Characterization of Content Traps in YouTube Recommendation Network

Md Monoarul Islam Bhuiyan*, Nitin Agarwal*†
*COSMOS Research Center, University of Arkansas at Little Rock, Arkansas, USA
†International Computer Science Institute, University of California, Berkeley, California, USA
e-mail: {mbhuiyan, nxagarwal}@ualr.edu

***Abstract*—YouTube's recommendation algorithm accounts for a substantial portion of total video views, influencing what users see and engage with. This study investigates how the algorithm may contribute to the formation of content traps, which are clusters of videos that repeatedly expose users to topically similar content. We employ Focal Structure Analysis (FSA), a Social Network Analysis (SNA) approach, to identify structurally cohesive groups of videos within the recommendation network, focusing on the China–Uyghur dataset as a case study. Topic modeling and divergence metrics are used to evaluate the thematic composition of each focal structure, revealing reduced topical diversity in areas where content traps are present. Building on this, we characterize each focal structure by its topical dominance, clustering coefficient, and the relative size of the focal structures, which allows us to distinguish between structurally dense traps and large, loosely connected ones. Our results show that content traps often exhibit strong topical alignment through tightly interconnected nodes. This study contributes a framework for identifying and characterizing content traps and offers insights relevant to understanding algorithmic reinforcement in content recommendation systems.**

Keywords-Content Traps*; *Characterization*; *YouTube Recommendation Network*; *Social Network Analysis.

I. INTRODUCTION

With the increasing influence of social media platforms, content sharing, news consumption, and community interaction have become deeply embedded in everyday digital behavior. YouTube, as the leading video-sharing platform and the second-most visited social media site globally, also plays a central role in this transformation. Operating in over 100 countries and 80 languages [1], YouTube's recommendation algorithm is responsible for 70% of the platform's watch time [2], making it a key driver of user engagement and content exposure. While this algorithm effectively suggests personalized content, it can also lead to the formation of content traps, which are sets of videos that repeatedly promote thematically similar material. This effect is especially concerning in sensitive domains, such as the China–Uyghur, where algorithmic patterns may amplify narrow topical exposure and limit access to diverse perspectives. Understanding how these traps form and persist is essential for evaluating the broader implications of recommendation systems [3].

In this study, we examine the emergence of content traps within YouTube's recommendation network by applying FSA [4], a Social Network Analysis (SNA) technique, to detect cohesive groups of nodes that may reinforce algorithmic exposure. We construct a directed graph based on video recommendation paths and identify focal structures that may act as attractor sets. To evaluate their thematic consistency, we apply topic modeling and measure Jensen–Shannon (JS) [5] and Kullback–Leibler (KL) [6] divergence scores between topic distributions, allowing us to quantify topical uniformity. These measures are particularly well-suited for evaluating topic concentration and distributional shifts in recommendation networks, where small differences in topic probability vectors may indicate the presence of algorithmic bias or thematic redundancy within focal structures. We further characterize each focal structure using structural features, such as average clustering coefficient and the relative size of the focal structures, enabling a multi-dimensional analysis of how content traps differ in form and scale. Thus, combining structural and semantic metrics contributes to a deeper understanding of content reinforcement in recommendation networks and its implications for algorithmic exposure.

To guide our investigation, we address the following research questions:

- **RQ1**. How can content traps be identified through focal structures within YouTube's recommendation network?
- **RQ2**. How can topic modeling and divergence metrics (JS/KL) be used to evaluate the topical consistency of focal structures?
- **RQ3**. How can content traps be characterized based on structural properties (e.g., average clustering coefficient, size) and topical dominance?

The remainder of this paper is structured as follows: Section II summarizes prior work on influential node detection and content traps in social media; Section III details our analytical approach; Section IV presents key findings; and finally Section V outlines implications and future directions.

II. RELATED WORK

This section is divided into two parts. First, we review methods for identifying influential nodes or sets of nodes in social networks. Then, we examine prior work related to content traps and content homogeneity in recommendation systems.

A. *Identifying Influential Sets in Social Networks*

Identifying structurally significant nodes or sets of nodes is central to Social Network Analysis. Classical methods, such as HITS [7] and PageRank [8] have measured node influence, while community detection techniques have aimed to group similar or densely connected nodes [9]. Moving beyond individual influence, recent work has focused on identifying smaller sets of key players that maximize information flow. FSA, introduced and extended in later studies [10], which identifies compact, relevant subgraphs overlooked by global centrality metrics. Alassad et al. [4] proposed a more comprehensive approach by combining user-level centrality with group-level modularity in a bi-level optimization framework to detect dense and sparse influential structures. Beyond detection, resilience and fragmentation metrics have been used to assess how these structures influence overall network stability [11].

B. Content Traps and Topical Homogeneity

Recommendation algorithms can create content homogeneity, reinforcing user exposure to repetitive themes. This phenomenon, closely related to filter bubbles [12], has been observed in various platforms, such as Facebook [13], and during events like the 2018 Brazilian election [14]. Research has proposed mitigation strategies, including diversification algorithms and fairness-aware link prediction models [15]. In addition, tools have also been developed to raise user awareness of algorithmic bias and promote content diversity [16][17]. Despite these efforts, there remains a gap in systematically identifying and characterizing content traps which are defined here as topically consistent clusters of videos within YouTube's recommendation network. Prior studies have focused primarily on conceptual or behavioral dimensions with limited empirical frameworks. Our study addresses this gap by applying FSA to detect potential traps and by using topic modeling and divergence metrics to evaluate their topical uniformity and diversity. We further assess their structural role in network connectivity, contributing to a clearer understanding of algorithm-driven content reinforcement on large-scale platforms.

To the best of our knowledge, no prior work systematically detects content traps using both structural and topical analyses. In this study, we aim to fill that gap by applying FSA and divergence metrics to YouTube's recommendation network.

III. Methodology

This section outlines our systematic approach to analyzing the YouTube recommendation network, detecting focal structures, and evaluating the presence of content traps. We start by summarizing our approach in collecting data, dataset background, and building YouTube recommendation networks. After that, we present the network resiliency approach taken to rank key focal structures. In addition, we lay the foundation for the analysis of the topics using the BERTopic model. Lastly, this section explores several metrics to investigate the topical consistency across different topics within the focal structures.

A. Data Collection

The data collection process in this study was designed to systematically capture YouTube's algorithmic behavior through its 'watch-next' recommendations. In this study, we analyzed the China–Uyghur. Below, we provide background details for this context and the motivation for studying them.

1) China–Uyghur Dataset: The situation in Xinjiang centers on the challenges faced by the Uyghur Muslim minority, including cultural repression, ethnic marginalization, and state-driven policies [18]. Scholars have examined the dataset through multiple perspectives, such as identity politics, language regulation, interethnic relations, and movements for greater autonomy [19]. Between 2018 and 2022, the issue gained increased international attention due to growing concerns over human rights violations.

We selected the China–Uyghur dataset for its geopolitical and ideological relevance in examining algorithmic content amplifications and recommendation dynamics within the recommendation network.

2) Keyword Generation and Crawling: We began by organizing workshops with subject matter experts to develop a focused set of keywords associated with the China–Uyghur. These keywords were used as search queries on YouTube to collect an initial set of seed videos. Below is a listing that shows the selected keywords for the collection of our dataset.

- Penindasan/oppression + Uighur/Uyghur
- Kejam/cruel + Uighur/Uyghur
- Saudara muslim/muslim brother + Uighur/Uyghur
- Kalifah/caliph + Uighur/Uyghur
- Khilafah/caliphate + Uighur/Uyghur
- "China is Terrorist"; "Stop Genocide"; "Save Muslim Uyghur"
- "Get Out China"; "I Love Muslim Uyghur"; "Peduli Uyghur" / "Care Uyghur"
- "Bebaskan muslim Uyghur dari penindasan China" / "Free Uyghur Muslims from China's oppression"
- "Do'a kan saudaramu" / Pray for Muslim Uyghur
- Hizbul Tahrir (HTI) + Uighur/Uyghur; Front Pembela Islam (FPI) + Uighur/Uyghur
- Nahdlatul Ulama + Uighur/Uyghur; Muhammadiyah + Uighur/Uyghur
- Hebibulla Tohti + Indonesia; Mohammed Salih Hajim + Indonesia
- Yusuf Martak + Uighur/Uyghur; Slamet Ma'arif + Uighur/Uyghur
- Xiao Qian + Uighur/Uyghur; Pendidikan/education + Uighur/Uyghur

We used a custom crawler to extract YouTube video recommendations up to five levels recursively, balancing data depth with computational feasibility [20][21]. Metadata and engagement statistics were collected via the YouTube Data API, while transcripts were obtained using an external method [22][23].

B. Recommendation Network Construction

The China–Uyghur dataset was constructed by initiating a recursive crawl starting from a curated set of seed videos that were retrieved using targeted keyword queries. YouTube's recommendation system was then used to capture up to four additional hops of recommended videos, resulting in a five-level directed network. This process yielded a graph consisting of 9,748 unique videos and 14,307 directed edges representing recommendation pathways. Our analysis was conducted on the recommendation graph, allowing us to examine how groups of interconnected videos that had contributed to patterns of topical consistency could be identified through focal structure analysis.

C. Focal Structure

Focal Structures (FSs) refer to distinct groups of nodes within a social network that play a central role in shaping influence or coordination. In the context of YouTube, we define focal structures as sets of videos that act as attractor content, potentially reinforcing specific themes and limiting exposure to diverse perspectives, thereby contributing to content traps.

We model the recommendation network as a graph $G = (V, E)$, where V represents videos and E denotes the recommendation links. Focal structures are defined as subgraphs $G' = (V', E')$, with $V' \subseteq V$ and $E' \subseteq E$, and are grouped into a collection $F = \{G'\}$. To ensure distinctiveness, no focal structure in F may fully contain another, i.e., for all $G_i, G_j \in F$, such that $i \neq j$, it holds that G_iG_j and G_jG_i [4]. This constraint guarantees that each focal structure represents a unique, non-overlapping attractor set suitable for analysis.

D. Network Resiliency Assessment

We conducted a network resilience analysis to evaluate the structural importance of focal structures within the recommendation network. Each focal structure was removed from the graph, and the number of resulting clusters measured the resulting network fragmentation. A greater number of disconnected components indicates that the removed structure played a central role in maintaining network cohesion. This method highlights the influence of focal structures in preserving content flow and structural integrity within the recommendation system [24].

E. Topic Modeling with BERTopic

We applied BERTopic [25] to video transcripts to uncover dominant themes associated with each focal structure. BERTopic was selected over traditional models like Latent Dirichlet Allocation (LDA) [26] for its ability to capture semantic and contextual nuances more effectively. Due to BERTopic's input size constraint (512 tokens), transcripts were split into coherent chunks along sentence boundaries. Topics were then mapped back to videos to analyze thematic distribution.

To identify content traps, we used a topic dominance threshold. If a single topic accounted for more than 50% of the videos in a focal structure, it was classified as a content trap. This condition is expressed as:

$$T = \frac{n_{topic}}{n_{total}} > 0.5 \tag{1}$$

where n_{topic} is the number of videos assigned to the dominant topic, and n_{total} is the total number of videos in the focal structure. This approach allowed us to identify clusters exhibiting low content diversity systematically.

F. Divergence Metrics

To further evaluate topical uniformity, we used two statistical measures, namely Kullback-Leibler (KL) Divergence and Jensen-Shannon (JS) Divergence, to compare topic distributions.

1) Kullback-Leibler (KL) Divergence: KL Divergence quantifies how one probability distribution diverges from a reference distribution:

$$D_{KL}(P||Q) = \sum_i P(i) \log \frac{P(i)}{Q(i)} \tag{2}$$

where P is the topic distribution of a focal structure and Q represents a uniform topical distribution across the topics of the focal structure. Lower values indicate higher similarity and, thus, stronger topical concentration.

2) Jensen-Shannon (JS) Divergence: JS Divergence is a symmetric, bounded variant of KL Divergence, defined as:

$$D_{JS}(P||Q) = \frac{1}{2}\left(D_{KL}(P||M) + D_{KL}(Q||M)\right) \tag{3}$$

$$M = \frac{1}{2}(P + Q) \tag{4}$$

A lower JS Divergence score similarly indicates high topic uniformity. KL and JS Divergence help quantify the degree of thematic consistency within focal structures.

In our analysis, low divergence values indicated content traps, while higher values suggested greater content diversity. These metrics offer a complementary quantitative basis for evaluating the presence of content traps in recommendation networks.

IV. Results

This section presents key factors contributing to content traps in YouTube's recommendation network. We begin by examining focal structures and their impact on network cohesion. We then assess KL and JS divergence metrics to evaluate topical consistency, and conclude by studying the identification and characterization of content traps through topic dominance and structural features.

A. Structural Role of Focal Structures in Network Connectivity

FSA is a network-based method aimed at identifying influential groups of nodes that collectively shape the structure and flow of information. In this study, we applied FSA to the recommendation network built from the China–Uyghur dataset and identified 105 focal structures. We removed each focal structure individually to evaluate its structural significance and analyzed the resulting network fragmentation. An increase in disconnected components following removal indicated a higher structural dependency on that focal structure. This process enabled us to determine the most critical structures supporting network cohesion, with the top five listed in Table I.

TABLE I: KEY METRICS FOR FOCAL STRUCTURES IN THE UYGHUR RECOMMENDATION NETWORK, INCLUDING SIZE, DOMINANT TOPIC, TOPIC UNIFORMITY, AND DIVERGENCE SCORES. STRUCTURES WITH UNIFORMITY ABOVE 50% ARE FLAGGED AS POTENTIAL CONTENT TRAPS.

Datasets	Focal Structure (FS)	No. Videos in FS	No. of Videos in Dominant Topic	No. of Clusters	Topic Uniformity	Content Trap	KL Divergence	JS Divergence
	3	105	64	185	61%	YES	0.680	0.158
	9	30	17	44	57%	YES	0.004	0.001
China-Uyghur	1	25	15	41	60%	YES	0.012	0.003
	102	13	7	31	54%	YES	0.067	0.234
	101	13	5	28	38%	NO	0.154	0.043

B. Topic Uniformity and Content Trap Identification in Focal Structures

To examine thematic concentration within the China–Uyghur recommendation network, we applied BERTopic to extract topics from video transcripts across the identified focal structures. Topic uniformity was measured by calculating the proportion of videos within each structure that shared the most dominant topic. A focal structure was classified as a content trap if over 50% of its videos aligned with a single topic. Focal Structures 3 (FS3) and 9 (FS9) met this criterion with other focal structures, with most of their videos associated with one dominant theme, indicating low topical diversity. This suggests that FS3 and FS9 may contribute to content traps by repeatedly exposing users to a narrow range of content. Table I reports the topic distribution statistics for FS3, FS9, and other key focal structures, while Figures 1 and 2 visualize the concentration of topics across the structure. These findings demonstrate how topic dominance within a focal structure can limit exposure to diverse content and reinforce algorithmically driven content loops, directly addressing **RQ1**.

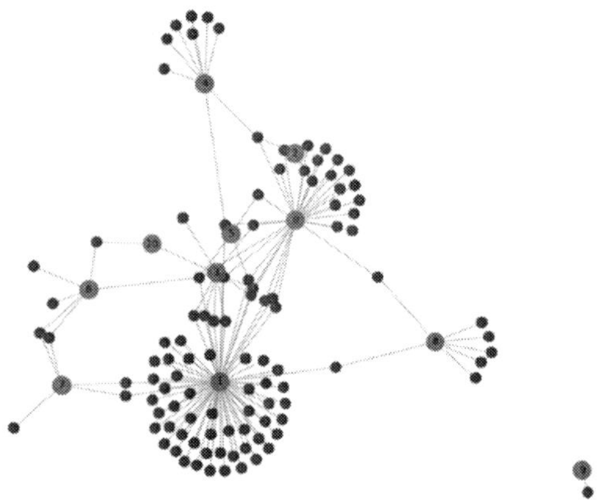

Figure 1: Network visualization of focal structure 3 in the China–Uyghur dataset, with red nodes as topics, blue nodes as video IDs, and edges indicating their associations.

C. Divergence Metrics and Their Role in Identifying Content Traps

In our study, we employed Jensen-Shannon (JS) and Kullback-Leibler (KL) divergence metrics to assess the topical consistency within focal structures. These measures quantify the similarity between topic distributions within a focal structure, which in turn helps us determine the presence of

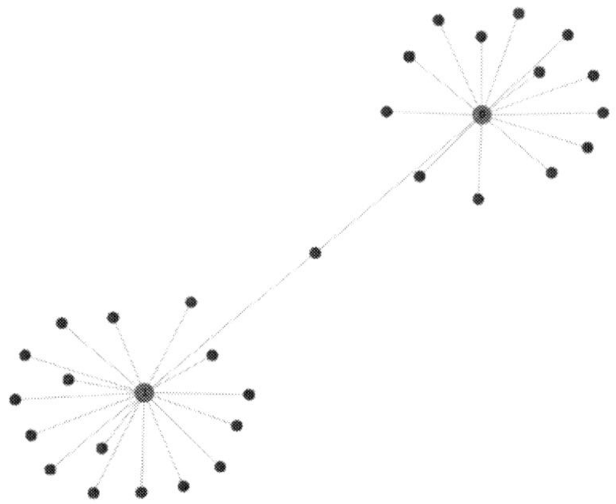

Figure 2: Network visualization of focal structure 9 in the China–Uyghur dataset, with red nodes as topics, blue nodes as video IDs, and edges indicating their associations.

content traps. Low divergence values indicate high topical uniformity, which suggests repetitive content exposure, while higher values reflect greater topic diversity.

Focal Structures 3 (FS3) and 9 (FS9) in the China–Uyghur dataset exhibited a relatively low JS divergence value alongside a moderately low KL divergence, indicating limited thematic variation across its constituent videos. This combination suggests that, although there is some distributional variability, FS3 and FS9 are still characterized by dominant topics that reduce content diversity. These metrics, reported in Table I, reinforce the classification of FS3 and FS9 as content traps, where algorithmic recommendations predominantly reinforce a narrow thematic scope. This finding contributes to our evaluation of **RQ2**, demonstrating how divergence metrics can reveal the extent of topic concentration within influential structures.

D. Characterizing Content Traps in Focal Structures

To understand the structural and topical properties of content traps within YouTube's recommendation network, we mapped each FS along two axes: topical dominance and either (i) average clustering coefficient or (ii) size, represented by the number of constituent nodes. This enabled a quadrant-based interpretation to characterize focal structures according to their structural cohesion and topical uniformity, both of which indicate their potential to function as content traps.

In the first analysis, as shown in Figure 3, we observe that Q1, representing focal structures with high topical dominance and average clustering coefficient, exhibits a dense aggregation

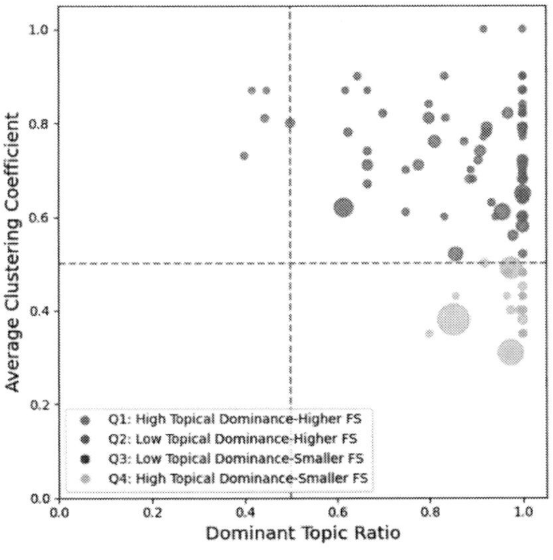

Figure 3: Characterization of content traps by dominant topic ratio and average clustering coefficient, illustrating structural and topical properties of focal structures.

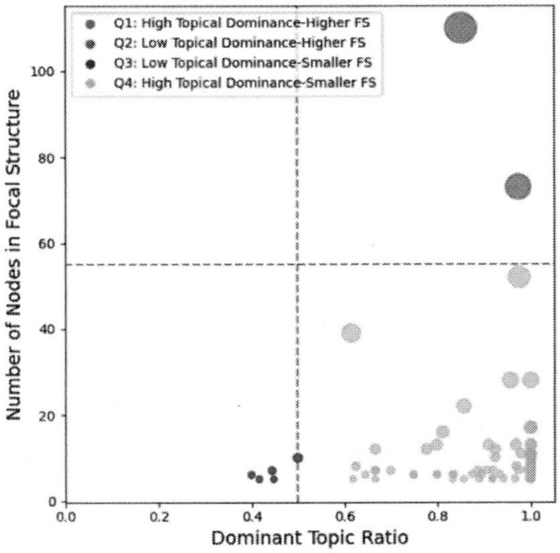

Figure 4: Content trap characterization by topic dominance and focal structure size.

of red-coded nodes. These structures are thematically uniform and structurally cohesive, forming tight-knit recommendation loops. Their high clustering suggests redundancy and limited escape routes for users, reinforcing their potential to function as strong content traps. Conversely, Q2 (low topical dominance, high clustering; green) reflects structurally dense but thematically diverse structures. These may serve as hubs of varied content but are less likely to trap users within a single narrative. Additionally, Q4 (high topical dominance, low clustering; orange) comprises topically consistent but loosely connected structures. Despite weak cohesion, some of the largest focal structures appear here, suggesting that scale and topical uniformity alone can sustain content traps. In other words, even without dense connectivity, large and uniform structures can act as broad-reaching traps. These may still act as traps due to content repetition with less structural reinforcement.

In the second analysis, as shown in Figure 4, we replace the clustering coefficient with the size of the focal structure to assess how node count interacts with topical dominance. Q1 again highlights high-risk traps: large, topically homogeneous structures dominate this quadrant. Their size and thematic alignment indicate both reach and reinforcing potential. In contrast, Q4 reveals numerous small, topically concentrated clusters, which may act as micro-traps that are limited in reach but still repetitive in exposure. Q2 is absent in this plot, reinforcing the rarity of large, thematically diverse structures. Q3 appears minimally, further supporting that small, diverse clusters are less likely to retain user attention. Together, these quadrant analyses suggest that content traps are best characterized by the convergence of structural density and topical uniformity, particularly in large focal structures. These insights support the development of targeted mitigation strategies that disrupt topical alignment (e.g., via content diversification) or structural reinforcement (e.g., reducing internal clustering). Furthermore, this structural–topical characterization lays the groundwork for interpreting how such traps may interact with user behavior, especially in the context of elevated engagement observed in high-uniformity structures, thus contributing to our understanding of **RQ3**.

V. Conclusion and Future Work

This study presented a network-based approach for identifying and characterizing content traps within YouTube's recommendation system, with a focus on the China–Uyghur context. By applying FSA, we extracted cohesive sets of videos that function as attractor content within the recommendation network. Through topic modeling and information divergence metrics (JS and KL), we evaluated topical uniformity across focal structures, revealing clusters with limited thematic variation. Our characterization further incorporated structural properties, such as clustering coefficient and size, enabling a nuanced understanding of how content traps differ in form and intensity. Engagement metrics provided additional support, highlighting user interactions that may reinforce the persistence of these traps. Our findings show that content traps are not solely defined by structural cohesion; even large, loosely connected focal structures can exhibit strong topical alignment and influence user navigation. This underscores the need to consider both network structure and content semantics in assessing algorithmic influence on content exposure.

Future work will focus on extending our analysis to include more network structure dimensions and content dimensions, and more topics/datasets/platforms to evaluate the generalizability of our findings. Additionally, we aim to compare our focal structure-based approach with other SNA methods to effectively identify content traps. We plan to integrate semiotic analysis [27] to examine how symbols impact the formation and reinforcement of content traps, and to explore content infusion strategies as a means of mitigating these effects.

ACKNOWLEDGEMENTS

This research is funded in part by the U.S. National Science Foundation (OIA-1946391, OIA-1920920), U.S. Office of the Under Secretary of Defense for Research and Engineering (FA9550-22-1-0332), U.S. Army Research Office (W911NF-23-1-0011, W911NF-24-1-0078), U.S. Office of Naval Research (N00014-21-1-2121, N00014-21-1-2765, N00014-22-1-2318), U.S. Air Force Research Laboratory, U.S. Defense Advanced Research Projects Agency, the Australian Department of Defense Strategic Policy Grants Program, Arkansas Research Alliance, the Jerry L. Maulden/Entergy Endowment, and the Donaghey Foundation at the University of Arkansas at Little Rock. Any opinions, findings, and conclusions or recommendations expressed in this material are those of the authors and do not necessarily reflect the views of the funding organizations. The researchers gratefully acknowledge the support.

REFERENCES

[1] C. Agency, *Youtube statistics*, *https://www.charleagency.com/articles/youtube-statistics/*, Accessed: April 10, 2025.

[2] A. Gallagher, L. Cooper, R. Bhatnagar, and C. Gatewood, *Pulling back the curtain: An exploration of youtube's recommendation algorithm*, *https://www.isdglobal.org/isd-publications/pulling-back-the-curtain-an-exploration-of-youtubes-recommendation-algorithm/*, Accessed: March 17, 2025.

[3] M. I. Gurung, M. M. I. Bhuiyan, A. Al-Taweel, and N. Agarwal, "Decoding youtube's recommendation system: A comparative study of metadata and gpt-4 extracted narratives," in *Companion Proceedings of the ACM on Web Conference 2024*, 2024, pp. 1468–1472.

[4] M. Alassad, M. N. Hussain, and N. Agarwal, "Comprehensive decomposition optimization method for locating key sets of commenters spreading conspiracy theory in complex social networks," *Central European Journal of Operations Research*, vol. 30, no. 1, pp. 367–394, 2022.

[5] J. Lin, "Divergence measures based on the shannon entropy," *IEEE Transactions on Information theory*, vol. 37, no. 1, pp. 145–151, 1991.

[6] S. Kullback and R. A. Leibler, "On information and sufficiency," *The annals of mathematical statistics*, vol. 22, no. 1, pp. 79–86, 1951.

[7] J. M. Kleinberg, "Authoritative sources in a hyperlinked environment," *Journal of the ACM (JACM)*, vol. 46, no. 5, pp. 604–632, 1999.

[8] S. Brin and L. Page, "The anatomy of a large-scale hypertextual web search engine," *Computer networks and ISDN systems*, vol. 30, no. 1-7, pp. 107–117, 1998.

[9] P. Bedi and C. Sharma, "Community detection in social networks," *Wiley interdisciplinary reviews: Data mining and knowledge discovery*, vol. 6, no. 3, pp. 115–135, 2016.

[10] F. Şen, R. Wigand, N. Agarwal, S. Tokdemir, and R. Kasprzyk, "Focal structures analysis: Identifying influential sets of individuals in a social network," *Social Network Analysis and Mining*, vol. 6, pp. 1–22, 2016.

[11] M. J. Alenazi and J. P. Sterbenz, "Comprehensive comparison and accuracy of graph metrics in predicting network resilience," in *2015 11th international conference on the design of reliable communication networks (DRCN)*, IEEE, 2015, pp. 157–164.

[12] E. Pariser, *The filter bubble: How the new personalized web is changing what we read and how we think*. Penguin, 2011.

[13] A. Bechmann and K. L. Nielbo, "Are we exposed to the same "news" in the news feed? an empirical analysis of filter bubbles as information similarity for danish facebook users," *Digital journalism*, vol. 6, no. 8, pp. 990–1002, 2018.

[14] G. M. Lunardi, G. M. Machado, V. Maran, and J. P. M. de Oliveira, "A metric for filter bubble measurement in recommender algorithms considering the news domain," *Applied Soft Computing*, vol. 97, p. 106771, 2020.

[15] F. Masrour, T. Wilson, H. Yan, P.-N. Tan, and A. Esfahanian, "Bursting the filter bubble: Fairness-aware network link prediction," in *Proceedings of the AAAI conference on artificial intelligence*, vol. 34, 2020, pp. 841–848.

[16] A. Amrollahi, "A conceptual tool to eliminate filter bubbles in social networks," *Australasian journal of information systems*, vol. 25, pp. 1–16, 2021.

[17] L. Burbach, P. Halbach, M. Ziefle, and A. Calero Valdez, "Bubble trouble: Strategies against filter bubbles in online social networks," in *Digital Human Modeling and Applications in Health, Safety, Ergonomics and Risk Management. Healthcare Applications: 10th International Conference, DHM 2019, Held as Part of the 21st HCI International Conference, HCII 2019, Orlando, FL, USA, July 26–31, 2019, Proceedings, Part II 21*, Springer, 2019, pp. 441–456.

[18] A. M. Dwyer, "The xinjiang conflict: Uyghur identity, language policy, and political discourse," *Policy Studies*, vol. 15, 2005.

[19] R. Hasmath, "What explains the rise of majority–minority tensions and conflict in xinjiang?" *Central Asian Survey*, vol. 38, no. 1, pp. 46–60, 2019.

[20] M. C. Cakmak, O. Okeke, U. Onyepunuka, B. Spann, and N. Agarwal, "Investigating bias in youtube recommendations: Emotion, morality, and network dynamics in china-uyghur content," in *International Conference on Complex Networks and Their Applications*, Springer, 2023, pp. 351–362.

[21] M. C. Cakmak, N. Agarwal, and R. Oni, "The bias beneath: Analyzing drift in youtube's algorithmic recommendations," *Social Network Analysis and Mining*, vol. 14, no. 1, p. 171, 2024.

[22] Google Developers, *YouTube Data API*, https://developers.google.com/youtube/v3, Accessed: April. 10, 2025.

[23] M. C. Cakmak and N. Agarwal, "High-speed transcript collection on multimedia platforms: Advancing social media research through parallel processing," in *2024 IEEE International Parallel and Distributed Processing Symposium Workshops (IPDPSW)*, 2024, pp. 857–860. DOI: 10.1109/IPDPSW63119.2024.00153.

[24] M. M. I. Bhuiyan, S. Shajari, and N. Agarwal, "Resilience and node impact assessment in youtube commenter networks leveraging focal structure analysis," *The Eleventh International Conference on Human and Social Analytics (HUSO 2025)*, 2025.

[25] M. Grootendorst, "Bertopic: Neural topic modeling with a class-based tf-idf procedure," *arXiv preprint arXiv:2203.05794*, 2022.

[26] D. M. Blei, A. Y. Ng, and M. I. Jordan, "Latent dirichlet allocation," *Journal of machine Learning research*, vol. 3, no. Jan, pp. 993–1022, 2003.

[27] M. I. Gurung, N. Agarwal, and M. M. I. Bhuiyan, "How does semiotics influence social media engagement in information campaigns?" In *Proceedings of the 58th Hawaii International Conference on Systems Science (HICSS-58)*, Big Island, Hawaii: Hawaii International Conference on System Sciences, Jan. 2025, pp. 6474–6483.